CW01262650

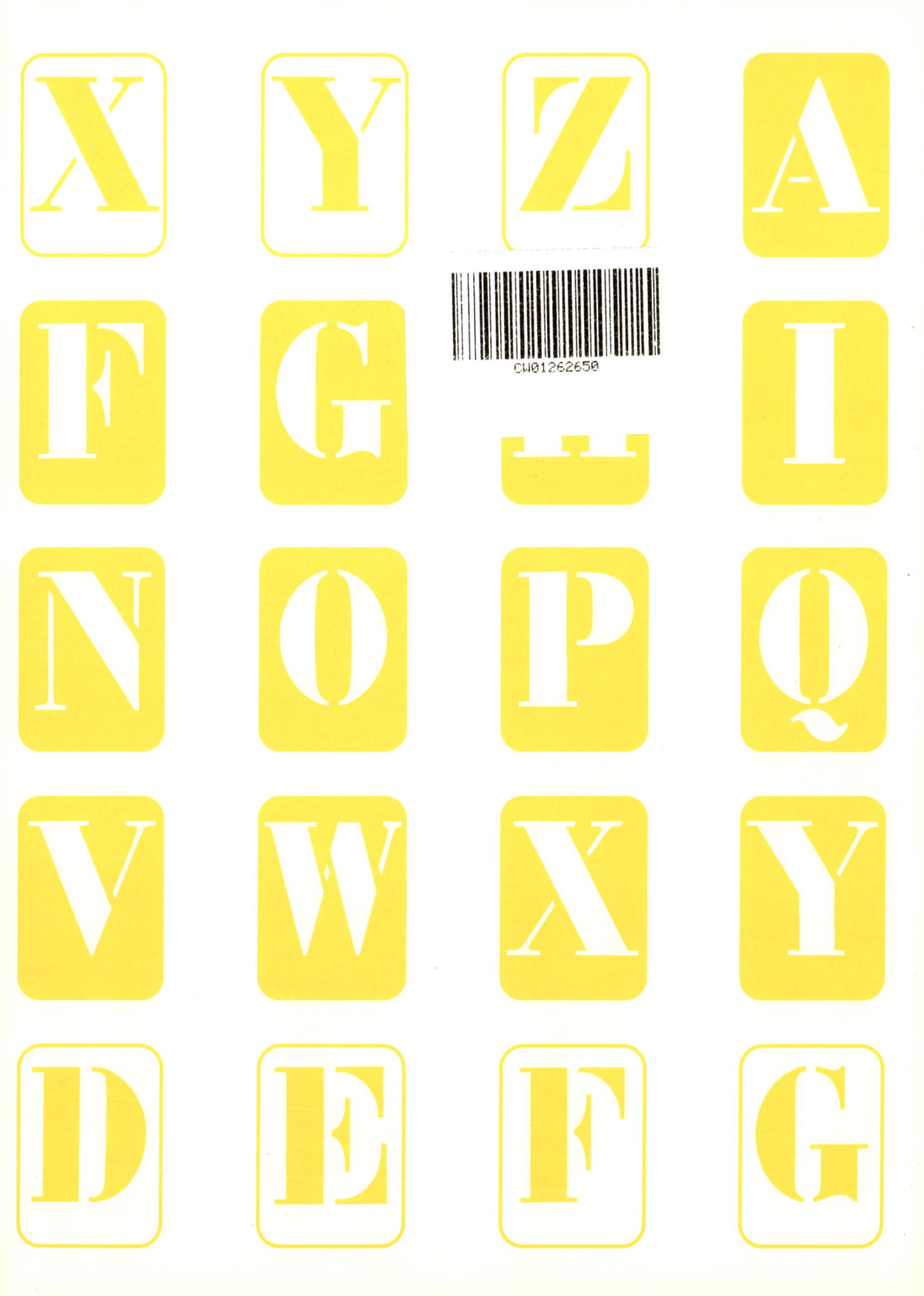

an alphabet of architectural models

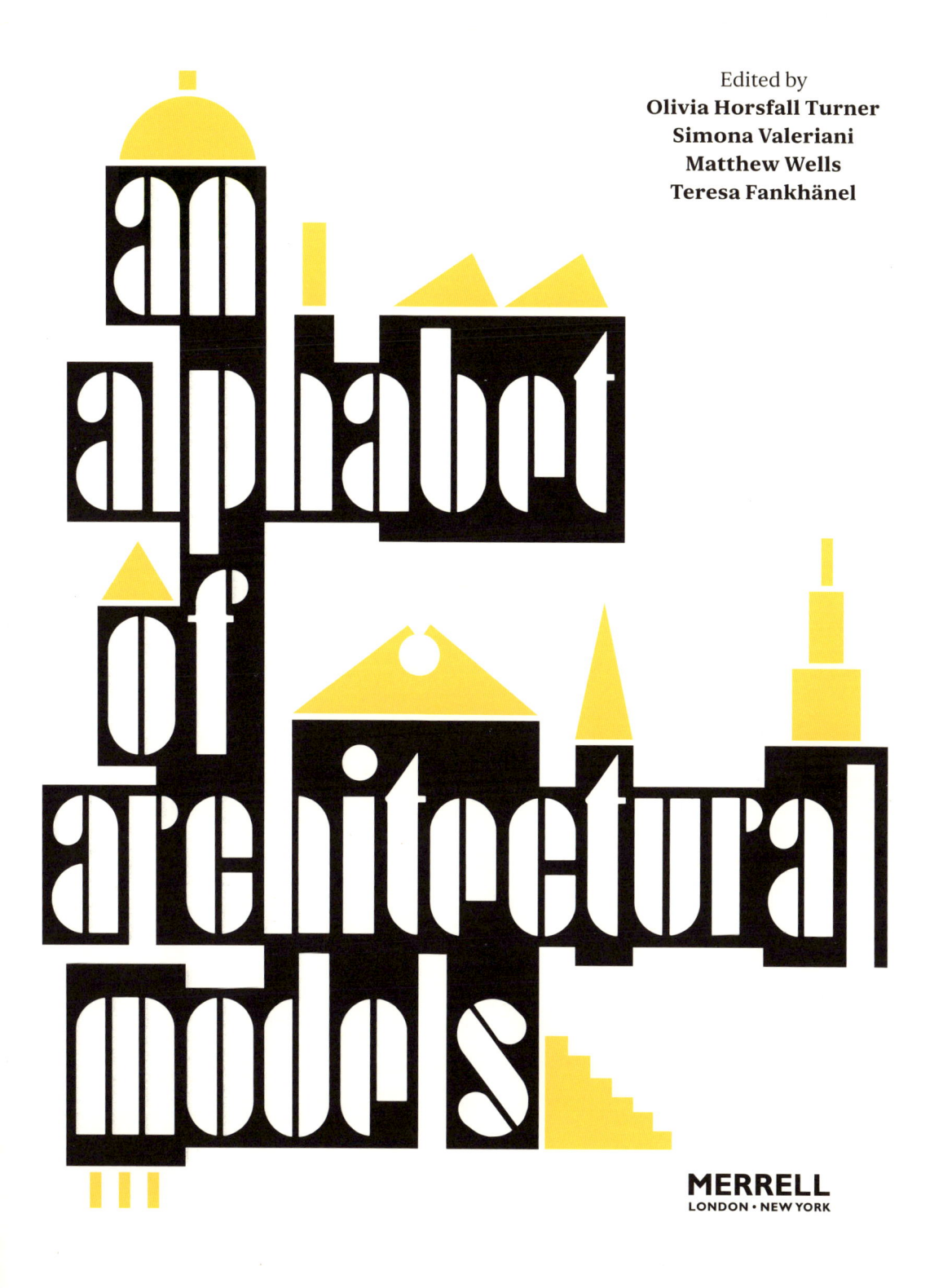

Edited by
Olivia Horsfall Turner
Simona Valeriani
Matthew Wells
Teresa Fankhänel

MERRELL
LONDON · NEW YORK

CONTENTS

4
Introduction
*Olivia Horsfall Turner, Simona Valeriani,
Matthew Wells and Teresa Fankhänel*

13
A for Ancient
Ulrike Fauerbach

17
B for Building
Biba Dow and Alun Jones

21
C for Cork
Helen Dorey

25
D for Digital
Angel Fernando Lara Moreira

29
E for Exhibition
Spencer de Grey

33
F for Film
Sarine Waltenspül

37
G for Gypsum
Mari Lending

41
H for Hand
Oliver Elser

45
I for Inspiration
Roz Barr

49
J for Junk
Martin Hartung

53
K for Kit
Vanessa Norwood

57
L for Landscape
Isabelle Warmoes

61
M for Making
George Rome Innes

65
N for Narrative
Nikos Magouliotis

69
O for One to One
Mary S. Morgan

73
P for Paper
Giovanni Santucci

77
Q for Quick
Rawden Pettitt

81
R for Representation
Ralf Liptau

85
S for Simulation
Hermann Schlimme

89
T for Toys
Charles Hind

93
U for Urban
Patrick Mckeogh

97
V for Virtual
ScanLAB Projects

101
W for Wood
Barnabas Calder

105
X for X-ray
Lisa Nash

109
Y for Yummy
Mark Morris

113
Z for Zoom
Davide Deriu

117 **Select Bibliography** 121 **Biographies** 126 **Index**

Introduction

*Olivia Horsfall Turner, Simona Valeriani,
Matthew Wells and Teresa Fankhänel*

Model for the Royal Albert Hall, London, showing the interior layout and decorative scheme, presented for Queen Victoria's approval in 1865.

Architectural models have many manifestations. Each and every stage of the design process can be embodied in three-dimensional form: from sketch models thrown in the dustbin, through concept models that are the touchstone for a project and 1:1 scale models that resolve a particular challenge in detail, to presentation models that capture the imagination of a patron and record models that retrospectively assert the logic and completeness of a scheme. Architectural models have been built from every type of material, from wood, clay, plaster, paper and card to metal, plastics and even food. With the advent of digital technology, modelling has developed to include computer-aided design (CAD) and, most recently, virtual reality, opening up new definitions of what an architectural model can be and how it might relate to our physical world. The life of the architectural model is not confined to the design studio: models are found in homes, schools and museums, and are valued for their didactic ability to convey ideas and demonstrate concepts in as clear a way as possible. Their image, too, is ubiquitous, multiplied and projected in photographs

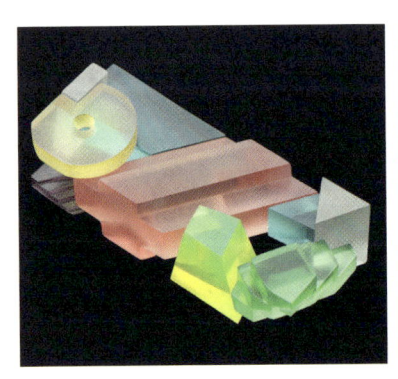

Reconfigurable cast-resin concept model of 2014 by Atelier La Juntana for the Ku.Be House of Culture and Movement, Frederiksberg, Copenhagen, by ADEPT and MVRDV.

The 'Great Model' (1673–74) for St Paul's Cathedral, London, built on a scale of 1:25, originally painted, and designed to be walked through at eye level.

and films, whether in order to record their appearance for posterity or to conjure up an alternative reality.

The use of three-dimensional models dates back thousands of years. Miniature representations of buildings and design models are known from ancient Egypt and Greece, and in his treatise *De architectura*, written in the first century BCE, Vitruvius documented the use of models in the design process. The architect and architectural theorist Leon Battista Alberti considered their advantages and disadvantages in detail in *De re aedificatoria* (1452), arguing that the use of models alongside drawings permitted the architect to refine a project to perfection. In the model, he explained, 'you may easily and freely add, retrench, alter, renew, and in short change everything from one end to the other, till all and every one of the parts are just as you would have them, and without fault'.[1] The model allowed any mistakes to be made at a manageable and affordable scale, and thereby encouraged deliberation and experimentation, and strengthened the overall design. Models made by builders also helped architects to test their theoretical ideas in practice. Such was the case when Sir Christopher Wren asked bricklayers to make a model of his design for the dome of St Paul's Cathedral, London, 'in small bricks' to establish its viability.

As well as the benefits that they offer to the architect, models have long been regarded as the most comprehensive and comprehensible form of architectural communication between architects, clients and craftsmen. The advantages of models to a wide range of observers were eloquently summarized by the British amateur architect Sir Roger Pratt, writing in 1660. Whereas all types of drawings, he explained, whether plans, elevations, sections or perspectives, 'do only superficially and disjointedly represent unto us the several parts of a

Model in hand-whittled bamboo by IBUKU design practice for Sharma Springs residence, Bali (2011), used to inform technical drawings and employed on site during building.

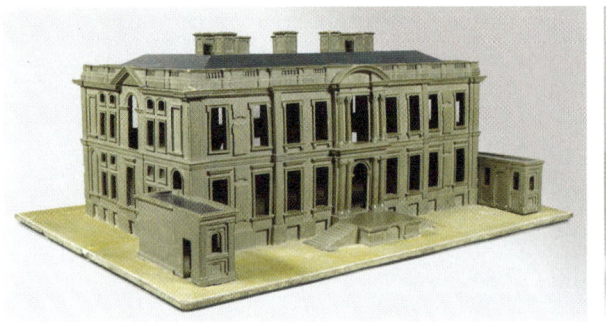

Model for Easton Neston, Northamptonshire, designed by Nicholas Hawksmoor c. 1690, containing a lift-out interior showing staircases, chimney breasts, columns, niches and plasterwork.

Paper model, made c. 1804 by Pierre-François-Léonard Fontaine, that can be folded to create a complete impression of the decorative scheme for a bedroom or cabinet.

building, a model does it jointly, and according to all its dimensions'.[2] This made a model more readily understood by a layperson, who might not have the necessary skill and experience to interpret technical drawings and projections.

    The legibility of models and their alleged lack of ambiguity also led to their recommendation as a sort of three-dimensional contract between architect and client. Pratt asserted that the use of a model in the commissioning of a building would avoid 'complaints' from patrons and 'abuse' from architects.[3] This idea was echoed in the nineteenth century by commentators who stressed that a model offered the most faithful representation of a building, because it offered the possibility of multiple points of view. As one journalist explained, 'The spectator can walk round, see it on every side, come close, and look into the little porches and recesses; go back and see the general appearance, move his eye along and judge of the effect of the altering perspective; and, if it will help him, raise himself and take a bird's-eye view of the roof'.[4] If models presented the truth to the viewer, one commentator argued that they could also achieve something yet more remarkable: they could 'render self-deception on the part of the architect impossible'.[5] Thanks to the perceived reliability of models, Sir John Soane even used them as evidence to prove his position in a legal case – an application for architectural models that has continued in modern practice, from investigations into Reactor 4 at the Chernobyl Nuclear Power Plant to the Grenfell Tower Inquiry.

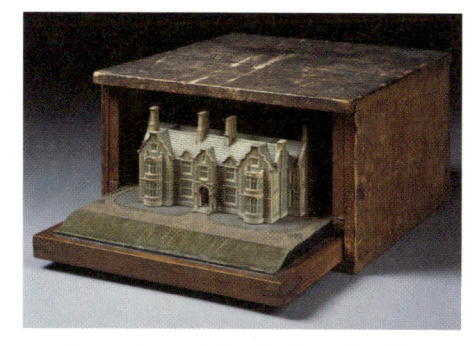

Presentation model for Pitt House, Chudleigh Knighton, Devon (1841), with its own travelling case to ensure safe delivery to the client, Thomas Pinsent.

The fidelity of models, however, has never been incontrovertible. In the same way that perspective drawings can deceive the viewer with an alluring interpretation of reality, it has to be admitted that models can also mislead, through their selective inclusion or exclusion of context, their use of materials or their photographic representation. Indeed, the ability of a model to usurp reality can be one of its strengths; this is the very premise on which architectural models are used to stand in for a city skyline in a film, to represent a novel feat of engineering or to conjure up a yet-to-be-constructed dream home in an advertising brochure. The seductive nature of such an alternative reality has, time and again, proven to be influential in changing the built environment.

John Soane used this wooden model of his house at 13 Lincoln's Inn Fields, London, in court in 1812 to defend his right to extend the façade.

Architectural models are capable of transporting the viewer to different places and to different times. This ability underpins their popularity not only in the context of practical

Plaster model of an unrealized proposal of 1925 for a tower to be built over Selfridges department store, London.

building projects but also as objects of decoration. In the late eighteenth century, wealthy young men in Europe undertook extended periods of travel and study in the Mediterranean and Middle East, in what became known as the Grand Tour. They brought back cork and plaster models of ancient sites for display as markers of their cultural experience and aesthetic sophistication. With the growth of popular travel, souvenirs in the form of mass-produced architectural ornaments or snow globes have performed the same function for a broader audience. Most recently, in a subversion of the collection of models for their positive associations, the designer Constantin Boym has produced the 'Buildings of Disaster' series (begun 1997) – tiny replicas of buildings that are linked to tragedy, catastrophe or scandal and that take their significance from these associations rather than from the buildings' aesthetic merit.

Model of Miyan Khan Chishti's Mosque, Ahmedabad, India, made in the mid-1800s and showing the building in its original form, before alterations of 1874 and repeated earthquake damage.

Model of pillars in Tirumala Nayak's Pudu Mandapa, Madurai, India, commissioned in the 1780s by a British surgeon in Madurai and sent to London to illustrate a 1789 report about Indian architecture to the Society of Antiquaries.

Plaster model of a tomb at Palmyra made in Paris by Jean-Pierre Fouquet c. 1820 and displayed during the 1820s and '30s in John Nash's Gallery of Architecture in London.

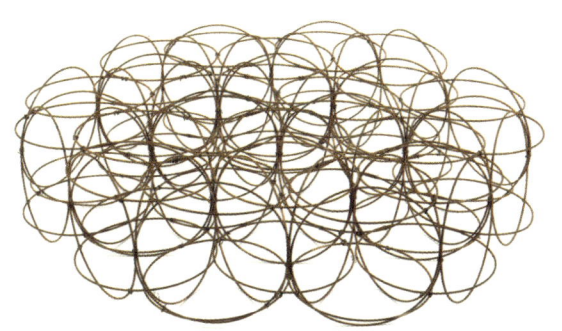

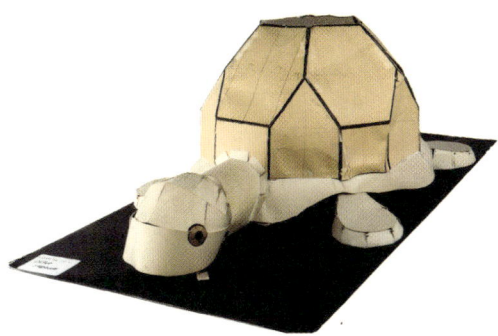

Hoop wire structural study of 1958–59 for the conceptual Ville Spatiale by Yona Friedman, proposing an infinite, mobile architecture.

Paper model for a pavilion in the shape of a tortoise (1972) by Jean Aubert, one of a series of ideas for zoomorphic inflatable structures.

The multiple forms and uses of models, combined with a fascination for the miniature, ignite interest in everyone who encounters an architectural model. It is their complexity and their capacity to provoke curiosity that underpin this collection of essays, written by model-makers, architects, curators, scholars and conservators. As editors, we wanted to find a format that would convey something of the variety and possibility of architectural models. The alphabet, containing the reconfigurable building blocks of words, offered a compelling structure. In addition, there is a long-standing tradition of designers conceiving of architectonic alphabets, as well as architects designing typographic alphabets themselves. Many of the initial letters featured in this volume are evidence of the creative resonance between the building blocks of language and the building blocks of architecture. It seems appropriate that models – which are the starting point for so many different ventures – should be represented through an alphabetical litany, each letter introducing one aspect of the architectural model's many lives. This book cannot offer a comprehensive account of the architectural model, but it runs the gamut of possibilities, and, we hope, will both enlighten readers and inspire further enquiry.

Cast-plaster model of 1950–51 for the south wall of the Chapelle Notre-Dame du Haut, Ronchamp, by Le Corbusier, expressing the sculptural quality of the finished building.

In **A is for Ancient**, Ulrike Fauerbach, Professor of the History of Architecture and Construction at the Ostbayerische Technische Hochschule Regensburg, introduces us to architectural models from ancient Egypt and classical antiquity, and explores what these artefacts tell us about their makers' creative and construction processes.

B stands for Building, in which Biba Dow and Alun Jones of Dow Jones Architects discuss their approach to model-making as a way of thinking that is the cornerstone of their architectural practice.

C is for Cork: From mass-produced souvenirs to bespoke teaching and learning tools, cork models have been produced and collected for centuries. Helen Dorey, Deputy Director and Inspectress of Sir John Soane's Museum in London, describes their significance.

Drawing on his experiences in both teaching and practice, Angel Fernando Lara Moreira, Head of Digital Prototyping at the Architectural Association in London, explores **D is for Digital** through the contemporary digital model, both as a prototyping tool and as a way of designing buildings.

The process of designing is a long journey, with abortive explorations and multiple revisions to achieve the final result. In **E is for Exhibition**, Spencer de Grey, Head of Design at Foster + Partners, gives an insight into the firm's attempt to reveal this process through exhibitions that demystify the many hours of work that go into design.

F stands for Film. Models have given film-makers the opportunity to make the impossible possible: to destroy, enter or manipulate buildings that are otherwise inaccessible to them. Sarine Waltenspül, postdoctoral researcher at the Zürcher Hochschule der Künste, looks at the way this has affected how films are made.

In **G is for Gypsum**, Mari Lending, Professor of Architectural History at the Oslo School of Architecture and Design, offers an insight into nineteenth- and early twentieth-century perceptions of models, particularly plaster casts as 1:1 scale models, through the imaginations of the writers Stendhal and Proust.

H is for Hand: Oliver Elser, Curator at the Deutsches Architekturmuseum in Frankfurt am Main, analyses how the architect's hand on the model symbolizes creation and control over an architectural design.

In a personal reflection on her own work, the architect Roz Barr considers **I for Inspiration**, in which she explores model-making as a highly creative process, led by materials, emotions and the subconscious.

J stands for Junk: Martin Hartung, doctoral fellow at ETH Zurich, takes a quick historical journey from the modern model's destruction to its rescue from the trash can as part of a growing awareness of preservation and market value.

From childhood toy to classroom equipment to the investigation of the ideal building unit, in **K is for Kit**, Vanessa Norwood, Creative Director of the Building Centre in London, explores model kits, and kits as models for contemporary and future building practice.

L is for Landscape, in which Isabelle Warmoes, Deputy Director of the Musée des Plans-Reliefs in Paris, presents the process and rationale behind the creation of *plans-reliefs*, models of towns and fortifications, between the seventeenth and nineteenth centuries. From measuring to describing, sketching and building, myriad landscapes took shape.

Based on his first-hand experience as model-maker in a variety of professional contexts over his long career, George Rome Innes reflects on **M is for Making**. Amid changing motivations, tools, materials and tastes, he considers what remains intrinsic to the art and science of model-making.

In **N stands for Narrative**, Nikos Magouliotis, doctoral fellow at ETH Zurich, considers the storytelling power of models through Conrad Schick's 1862 model of the Church of the Holy Sepulchre, which contained moveable, colour-coded parts to show the spatial and legal complexity of a building that was – and continues to be – owned and used simultaneously by different Christian denominations.

What do fruit flies, economic systems machines, pancake batter and balsa wood have in common? In **O is for One to One**, Mary S. Morgan, Albert O. Hirschman Professor of History and Philosophy of Economics at the London School of Economics, considers model-making, and the problems of scale connected to it, in the contexts of architecture and science.

P stands for Paper. Giovanni Santucci, research fellow in art history at the Università di Pisa, explores the uses of and roles played by paper models from sixteenth-century Italy until the modern period, and draws on a diverse range of examples, including wooden models lined with paper drawings and three-dimensional *modelli di cartone*.

Q is for Quick: Focusing on the work of Stanton Williams Architects, the architect Rawden Pettitt considers the role of the physical model as a way of thinking both quickly and slowly in a world of architectural practice that is increasingly virtual and mediated by technology.

In **R is for Representation**, the architectural historian Ralf Liptau looks at the model's ability to refer to things other than itself in light of its use as a design tool and its afterlife as a medium of presentation.

How do architects and architectural historians use digital modelling and simulations to understand the built environment? In **S is for Simulation**, Hermann Schlimme, Professor and Chair of History of Architecture and Urbanism at the Technische Universität Berlin, considers how the digital simulation of a lost industrial site designed by Hans Poelzig demonstrates the potential of digital models to re-create complex relationships within lost architectural compositions.

T is for Toys: Charles Hind, Chief Curator and H.J. Heinz Curator of Drawings at the Royal Institute of British Architects in London, reveals the history of architectural models as toys that have engaged and entertained children and adults from the late eighteenth century to the present day.

U stands for Urban: Patrick Mckeogh, Managing Director of Pipers Model Makers, draws on the vast experience of his family-owned company, which has produced models for decades, to explore the role of the context model and the urban model in the design process. What is the genuine context of a scheme? How can architects and developers engage with a wide range of stakeholders?

In **V is for Virtual**, members of ScanLAB Projects explain how, in architectural practice, the virtual plays an important role in materializing a dream, an idea, a concept. A virtual model can be accurate to the submillimetre. It can also defy the laws of physics that constrain the 'real', and blur the edges between this world and another.

W is for Wood: Drawing on his expertise of Brutalist architecture, Barnabas Calder, historian of architecture and energy at the University of Liverpool, uses the balsa-wood models made in-house by Denys Lasdun's model-maker to offer new insights into Lasdun's design process.

Looking at a model like a doctor looks at a patient, in **X is for X-ray**, Lisa Nash, Senior Conservator at the Royal Institute of British Architects, explains what different visualization techniques can reveal about the interior workings of a model. Through an in-depth understanding of their composition, she exposes their vulnerabilities and finds ways of prolonging their fragile lives.

In **Y is for Yummy**, Mark Morris, Head of Teaching and Learning at the Architectural Association, traces the history of edible architecture through scaled treats in the form of cakes, jellies and confectionery in literature, royal patronage and architectural practice.

Z stands for Zoom: Davide Deriu, Reader in Architectural History and Theory at the University of Westminster, examines the significant part played by photography in the production and reproduction of architectural models over the past 100 years, with reference to influential architects, unbuilt competitions and avant-garde artists.

NOTES

1. Leon Battista Alberti, *The Ten Books of Architecture: The 1755 Leoni Edition*, New York (Dover) 1986, Book II, Chapter I, p. 22.
2. R.T. Gunther (ed.), *The Architecture of Sir Roger Pratt*, Oxford (Oxford University Press) 1928, pp. 22–23.
3. *Ibid.*, p. 22.
4. 'Architectural Modelling', *The Building News*, vol. 14, 6 December 1867, p. 851. Quoted in Matthew J. Wells, 'Architectural Models and the Professional Practice of the Architect, 1834–1916', PhD thesis, Royal College of Art/Victoria and Albert Museum, London, 2019, p. 68.
5. 'Preliminary Studies', in *A Dictionary of Architecture and Building*, vol. 3, London (Macmillan) 1902, p. 208.

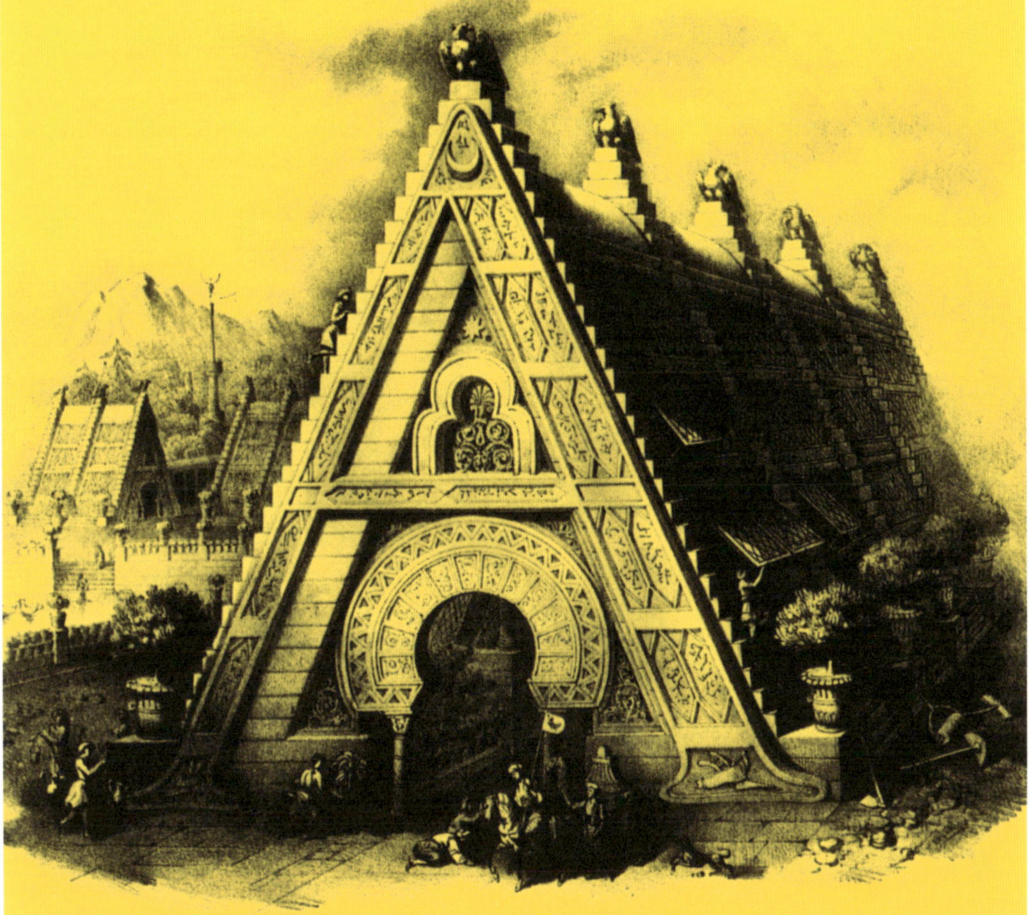

Ancient
Ulrike Fauerbach

Sources from the Middle East confirm that the technique of making models of buildings is almost as old as architecture itself, and goes back to the Neolithic period. These early models varied in terms of technique, subject matter and purpose, but they were often religious or symbolic in nature; even the oldest known model that was an architect's project dates back to the nineteenth century BCE.

Another surprising fact is the sheer mass of miniatures preserved from the eastern Mediterranean; they number in the high hundreds. The materials of which these surviving examples are predominantly made – terracotta and limestone – are long-lasting, and should remind us that other model-making materials are rarely found in archaeological contexts because they have decayed or been burned, melted or reused. A gap in our findings therefore needs to be taken into account. The functional variety of the models presents a further difficulty. It is useful to differentiate two categories, which we shall here call miniatures and models.

Miniatures are to be understood as scaled-down reproductions of such building types as domestic, public and cult buildings, or elements of them. We can learn about architectural features from these objects, but they could not be said to represent *particular* buildings; instead they depict houses, temples, towers and other forms *in general*. They are a by-product of architecture rather than a prerequisite for it, and embody an idea widely followed in antiquity: namely, that a miniature, non-functional object – for example, an ex-voto or a grave good – can magically represent the real thing.

Models, on the other hand, served as paradigms for actual structures. They were made to develop a design or to explain it to others, such as craftsmen or patrons. They can be of a reduced size, but we also know of the existence of full-scale models.

How can we tell one from the other? Many miniatures are easily recognized by their sketchy yet ornamental character and the frequent repetition of certain types, often with designs that do not correspond to the architectural reality of their time. The frequently found circular plan, for instance, came about only because of the production of miniatures on potter's wheels. Sometimes miniatures are inhabited by or decorated with human or divine figures or religious symbols. Others can be recognized by traces of having been used as urns or incense burners or for libations, or by being made of materials ill-qualified to display details.

Telltale features of models, on the other hand, are a contemporary design, a coherent scale, and guidelines or inscribed measurements. A focus on specific details or on a particular part of a building, and an overall unattractive appearance, may also be clues. The most common materials – such as limestone and, less often preserved, wood – could be sculpted easily and, importantly, could be handled comfortably on a building site.

The oldest known architectural model proper represents a sequence of passages and rooms inside a pyramid of the Egyptian king Amenemhat III, and dates to the nineteenth century BCE. The 72-centimetre-long (28½ in.), rather plain model was cut from a limestone slab. Its most interesting feature is a wooden sliding block representing the sealing plug of the burial chamber. Comparison with the pyramid to which it probably refers indicates that it was only a preliminary design. The model has no coherent scale and focuses on the spatial relation of the rooms and most prominently the blocking system, which was a major issue in royal tombs of that period.

A large group of Egyptian models, more than 100 in number, represent architectural details – mostly columns and their parts, but also door frames and gargoyles. The majority are made of limestone, are easy to handle because of their relatively small size, and have at least one of the following features: guidelines, variations of typological detail, and different working stages in one and the same piece. Their scale is usually coherent; there are even groups of several objects in the same scale. They date to ancient Egypt's Late Period, mostly to the second half of the first millennium BCE. From the late seventh century BCE, the changing architectural style challenged Egyptian master builders with the task of designing a variety of complex new forms, a development that explains the emergence of models of details. The oldest datable piece was found in the workmen's village of Deir el-Medina, and can be dated exceptionally early, to the eleventh or tenth century BCE.

Artefacts from ancient Greece differ in number and quality. Written sources mention *paradeigmata*, that is, models for communication between architects and patrons. They probably depicted not complete buildings, but architectural details. The use of scaled-down models of complete buildings was seemingly neither necessary nor useful: the strict compliance with typology and proportion resulted in mostly predefined measurements that in any event could not have been taken from scaled-down models accurately enough. In consequence, models of details at a 1:1 scale are more probable, and such *paradeigmata* have indeed been

Limestone model of an ancient Egyptian capital (4th–2nd century BCE) showing different working stages: on the left, the preparatory stage; on the right, the finished detailing.

substantiated. Around 360 BCE, the architect Polykleitos the Younger applied the then still new Corinthian order to the Tholos in Epidaurus. Within the temple a deliberately buried Corinthian capital has been found, perfectly executed but with minute variations in details. It is presumed to have been carved by Polykleitos himself as a model for his co-workers. On the island of Samos during the sixth century BCE, a certain Eupalinos produced an *in situ* full-scale model: a 5-metre-long (16½ ft) section of a water tunnel that served, according to the word *paradeigma* inscribed on the wall, as a prototype for the whole tunnel project.

Excavated capital (c. 360 BCE) from the Tholos in Epidaurus, believed to have been carved by the architect Polykleitos the Younger as a model for the masons.

Roman architecture was far less standardized than that of ancient Greece, a fact that rendered three-dimensional planning tools both useful and necessary. Next to the larger of the two temples in Niha, Lebanon, was found a model of part of this building at a scale of 1:24. Dating from the second century CE, it was made of limestone and may have had a wooden component, now lost, representing the façade. The preserved piece represents the stairway leading to the podium of the temple. The measurements inscribed on the steps are those of the actual building, and also indicate the alteration of details during the design process.

Another model from Lebanon, also representing stairs, was made to help design and communicate the Great Altar in the sanctuary of Jupiter Heliopolitanus in Baalbek. The altar has a monolithic aspect from the outside, but is, in fact, hollowed out by an intricate staircase. The object is thought to be only one fragment of a multitude of pieces that must have been necessary to plan one of the most complex buildings of the ancient world.

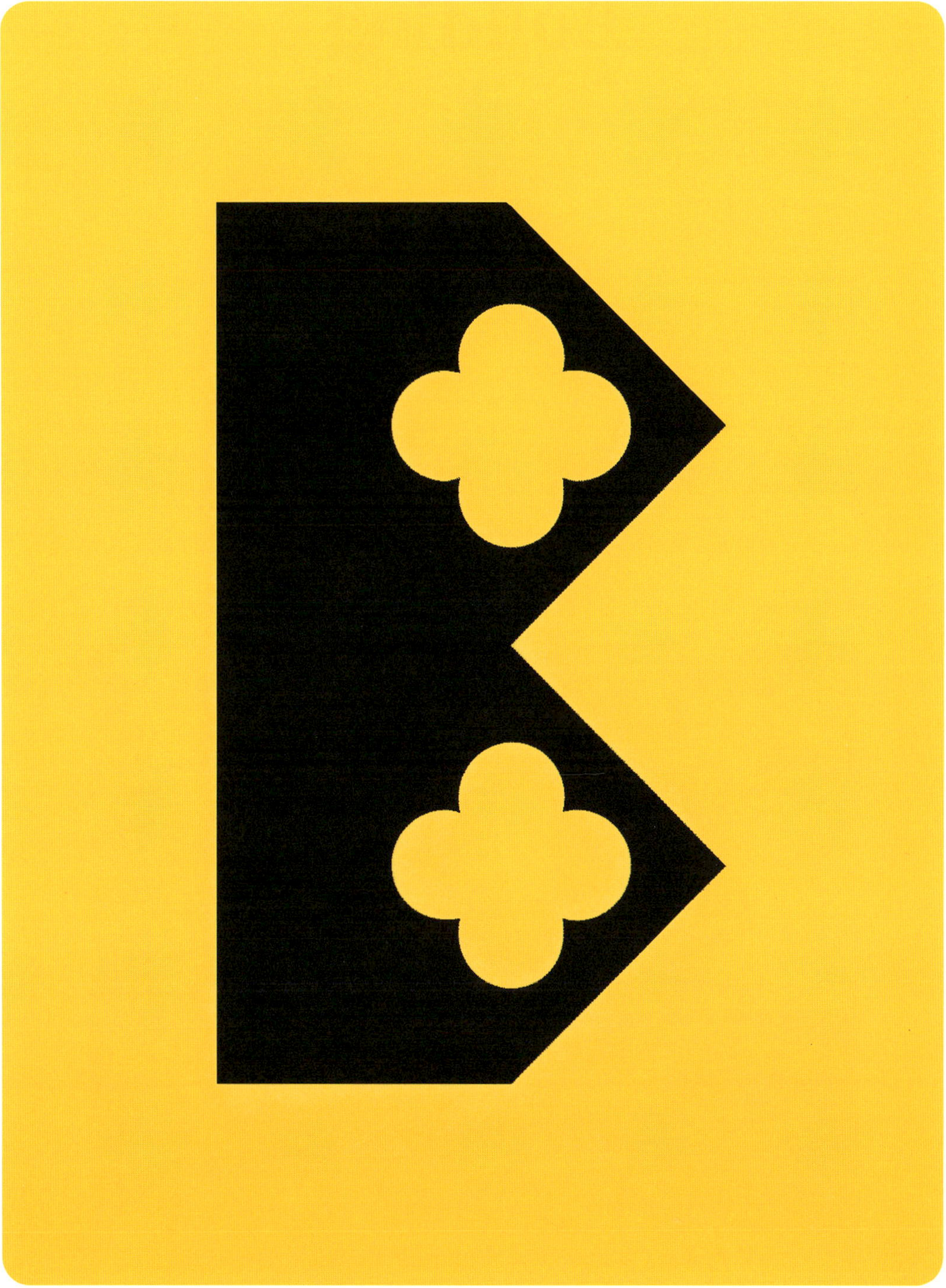

Building
Biba Dow and Alun Jones

Model-making forms the cornerstone of our practice. We make models for a number of reasons, at a variety of scales and with a range of techniques. We make models to bring conceptual ideas to visibility, to judge questions of form and scale, to test spatial proposals, to look at how light will fall into a room, and to assess how materials will sit one with the other; these fundamental questions apply to all scales and types of building. The model is used as a central design tool, and not as a means to show what a final design will look like. Models are most useful when they form part of an ongoing iterative process, made to explore a variety of questions.

The models we are talking about here are physical models, not computer-aided design (CAD) ones. In model-making we are looking for a tangible representation of spatial relationships and qualities of light and scale, and these are hard to convey convincingly in something that is immaterial. The physical model plays directly into

Model-making in the studio of Dow Jones Architects, showing a working model of St Anselm's Church, Kennington (2020).

Site model of the Garden Museum, Lambeth, by Dow Jones Architects, featuring patinated copper foil to emulate bronze tiles (2013).

the design process and allows for intuitive development; though they are quick to produce and capable of representing complexity, CAD models do not do this.

We follow a rough pattern, starting with a small-scale model and, as the design of a building progresses, increasing the scale, as the focus of the model becomes more specific. To explain conceptual ideas, we make models at small scale or not to scale at all. This sort of model might or might not look like the building, but will typically have a strong material or formal presence to encompass and bring visibility to the essential idea for the project. Cast plaster, raw timber, resin, gold leaf and beaten copper have all been used in this type of model. The purpose is to appeal to the imagination and be deliberately open-ended, but also to imply a material presence and to communicate an overarching idea about form and connections. It is an invitation to the viewer to participate. We often give these sorts of conceptual model to the client as something to hold and keep, as the genesis for the project, and to start a conversation; therefore, the feel of the model as a physical thing is important.

We make models at a scale of 1:200 or 1:100, depending on the size of the project, in order to explore ideas of form and relationship. These models look at the form of the proposal itself and also at the relationship with the building's context. This type of model will usually be made of grey packaging cardboard and will follow Leon Battista Alberti's advice in *De re aedificatoria* (1452), in which he recommends that models should not mislead the viewer by being coloured or materially representational, so that, as he says, the 'lineaments' of the design can be truly appreciated. Such models are quickly made and equally quickly remade – scalpel and glue replace the pencil – and natural light forms a key part of the process. The purpose of this type of model is to appeal to the eye and to exercise our judgement as part of refining the design. These models develop building ideas that have started as sketches. Making them as three-dimensional objects reveals very different things. We might photograph the models and also show them to people, but the principal purpose is to develop the design.

The next scale of model we make is 1:20, usually to explore interior spatial qualities and the way in which light falls on material and into a room. It will normally be made of foam board and will be clad with 'real' materials or representations of them. These models are generally not of a whole project; they might be of the corner of a room or a junction of spaces. We make them in order to look at the design in more detail and to photograph them, and the photograph is the principal outcome of this exercise. Photographing this type of model can take as long as making the model itself, and such models are inhabited by scale furniture, artworks and people printed on cardboard and cut out. The quality of real light making real shadows in these models is always going to be better than the Photoshop equivalent. The models themselves are fairly crude, as they are made to be seen from only one side, but the photographs of these spaces have real character.

We have also used the 1:20 scale model to explore cladding options. For our Garden Museum project in Lambeth (2013–17), we made a range of façade cladding options that looked at different arrangements of the bronze tiles. The model tiles were made of copper foil, which we patinated by rubbing lemon juice on it and heating it over the gas hob in the kitchen.

We sometimes make models at 1:1 scale to test the actual size of things. We made the faience tiles for the Grand Junction project at St Mary Magdalene's Church in Paddington (2010–19) in grey packaging cardboard at full size and placed them on the wall outside our office to review the depth of the relief pattern cast on to the cladding, observing how the sun would fall across the tiles at different times of the day.

The one sort of model we never make is what we refer to as a 'train set' model, which is a model made at the end of the design process to show, or prove, that you were somehow right all along.

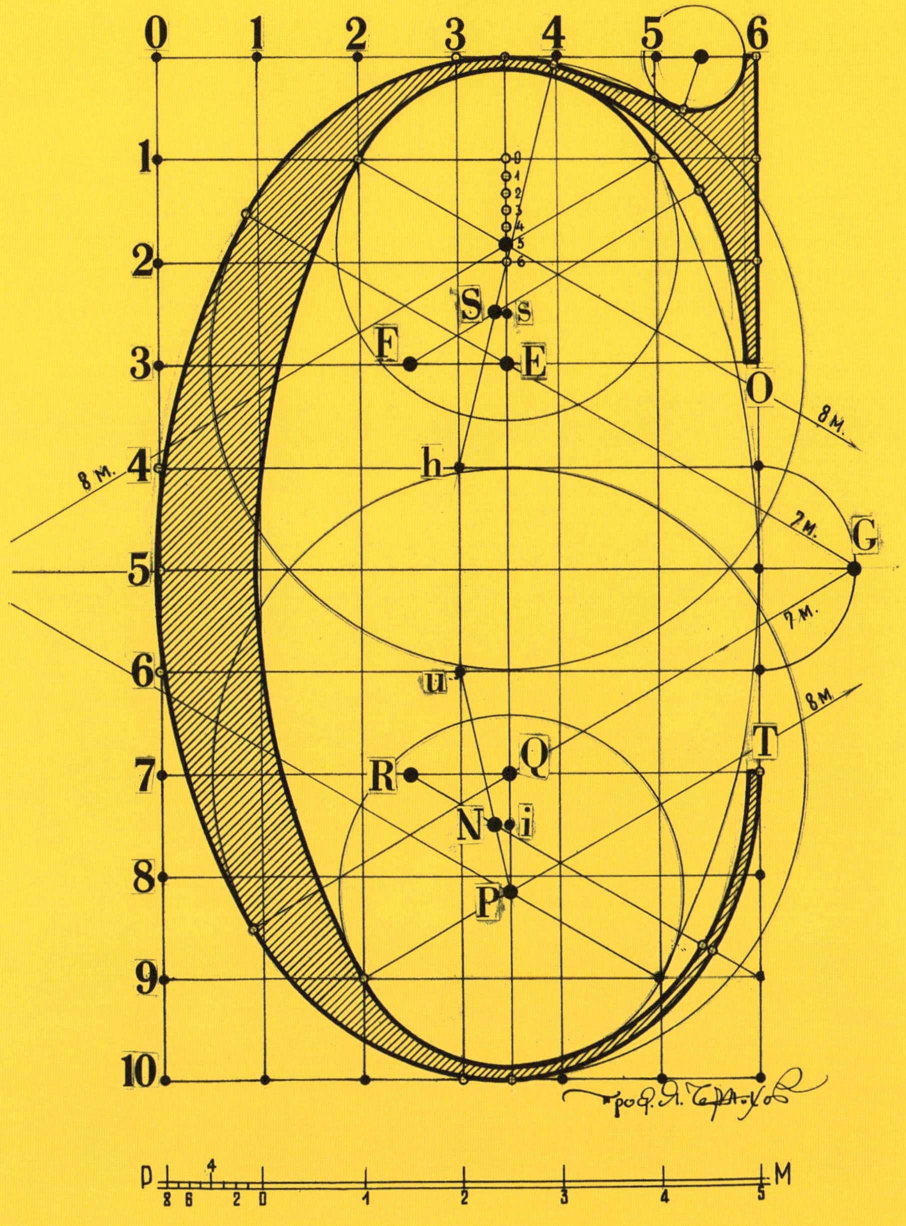
0 1 2 3 4 5 6
1 2 3 4 5 6 7 8 9 10
S s F E O h G u Q R N i P T
8 м.
7 м.
проф. Я. Чернихов
P M
8 6 2 0 1 2 3 4 5

Cork

Helen Dorey

Cork, the bark of the cork oak tree (*Quercus suber*), has been exploited by man since ancient times. It was used by the ancient Egyptians and Romans for the soles of shoes and, during the Middle Ages, as an insulating material for monastic cells. Cork is naturally durable, easy to carve and available in different thicknesses and qualities. It is very stable and able to adapt to variations in temperature and pressure without distorting. Thanks to the suberin and ceroids in its cell walls, it is practically impermeable to liquids and gases, while its resistance to moisture enables it to age without deteriorating. It is slow to conduct heat and resistant to abrasion. These characteristics make it ideally suited for the making of architectural models.

Engraved view of Sir John Soane's Model Room at 13 Lincoln's Inn Fields, plate XXXVIII from Description of the Residence of Sir John Soane, Architect *(1835), showing the model-stand with numerous cork and white plaster models.*

The origin of the use of cork for modelling probably lies in the tradition of making *presepi*, or Christmas cribs, in southern Italy, particularly Naples, in which cork from local oak woods was used, together with other materials, to create the elaborate architectural settings for nativity scenes. In the sixteenth century Giorgio Vasari recorded the existence of a cork model of Florence commissioned by Pope Clement VII and manufactured from measurements taken in secret before it was smuggled out of the city to be used in the planning of a papal military campaign. This seems to be the earliest known 'proper' architectural model in cork.

By the late eighteenth century, cork was being widely used to depict ancient structures in

Cork model of the Temple of Vesta at Tivoli, near Rome, made by Giovanni Altieri in the 1770s and visible in the 1835 engraving of Soane's Model Room (opposite).

their contemporary ruined state. The colour and honeycomb cellular structure of the material meant that it could be brilliantly deployed to portray crumbling and decaying structures while itself being the opposite. The growth of interest in excavating, surveying and studying sites led to a parallel desire to record them accurately in three-dimensional, rather than just two-dimensional, form. The museum in Naples founded in 1777 (today the Museo Archeologico Nazionale di Napoli), for example, commissioned models of the site of Pompeii. Cork models also came to be highly desirable souvenirs for those making the 'Grand Tour' – a journey around Europe, usually to Italy, undertaken by well-born young gentlemen to complete their education – and commanded high prices. Cork was exceptionally light, making it easy to transport home.

From the 1760s, named makers were producing cork models that found their way into collections across Europe. Agostino Rosa (1738–1784) and Antonio Chichi (1743–1816) were trained architects who also produced a repertoire of cork models of celebrated Roman buildings. Chichi's clients included Catherine the Great (the models she purchased are at the Russian Academy of Arts in St Petersburg) and German princes. His models can be seen at the Hessisches Landesmuseum Darmstadt, the Herzogliches Museum Gotha and the Akademie der Künste in Berlin. During a trip to Italy in 1777, Friedrich II, the Landgrave of Hesse-Kassel, ordered a series of thirty-six buildings, which were delivered in 1782. Thirty-three can still be seen at Schloss Wilhelmshöhe in Kassel. Giovanni Altieri (*fl.* 1767–1790) came from Naples, although he spent seventeen years working in Rome. He made a number of models for English clients. Sir William Hamilton, British Envoy to the Kingdom of Naples, reportedly commissioned Altieri to make a large model of Vesuvius for King George III, but there is no evidence that the model was completed. Model-makers outside Italy, such as Richard Du Bourg in London and Carl and Georg May in Germany, made and sold cork models in their own countries. Many were acquired by museums and institutes for didactic purposes and were displayed alongside drawings and collections of antiquities.

The English architect Sir John Soane (1753–1837) acquired fourteen cork models from different sources. The majority, including a plan model of Pompeii as it was in 1820 and models of the Doric temples at Paestum, were made in the early nineteenth century by a Naples-based model-maker named Domenico Padiglione. They were bought in Italy by John Sanders, who had been Soane's first architectural pupil in the 1780s. After Sanders's death, Soane bought them at Christie's in 1826. He commissioned a large model-stand and between 1834 and 1835 created an elaborate Model Room in which his collection of cork models (the largest such collection in the UK) was displayed alongside white plaster models of ancient buildings 'reconstructed' and models of his own projects.

Cork is best known today for its use in the wine industry, for flooring and as the core of cricket balls. The fashion for making architectural models in cork waned during the late nineteenth and early twentieth centuries, and many were destroyed or disposed of by institutional owners as teaching methods changed. However, cork is clinging on as a modelling material. It continues to be seen stacked up outside the shops of *presepe*-makers in via San Gregorio Armeno, Naples, and small-scale, crude models are still sold to tourists at sites in Sicily.

Only one man, in Germany, has made it his mission to continue creating exquisite models in the manner of the eighteenth-century masters. Since the 1980s Dieter Cöllen has been studying the art of phelloplasty (cork model-making). He develops his models through study of the ruins themselves and analysis of drawings and engravings, but he also, in his own words, bases them 'on scientific foundations, on the latest discoveries and research by the archaeologists and architectural historians I collaborate with', combined with the highest standards of craftsmanship and artistry. This combination enabled the re-creation of the missing half of Padiglione's model of the ruins of Pompeii (disposed of in the 1890s to reduce its size for convenience) for the Model Room at Sir John Soane's Museum. On this project, Cöllen collaborated with the world's foremost expert on cork models, Valentin Kockel, an archaeologist who has also worked at Pompeii over a number of decades.

Cöllen's latest project is to make a cork model of the city of Palmyra in Syria, showing its condition before its destruction by ISIS militants in 2015. His ultimate aim is an exhibition that 'reveals the momentous changes of our time and enables viewers to comprehend these emotionally'. His work is testament both to the appropriateness of cork for creating archaeologically accurate records of the state of ancient buildings and to the emotional power of the cork model, not only in the eighteenth century as one of the most evocative and romantic of all Grand Tour souvenirs, but also today.

D

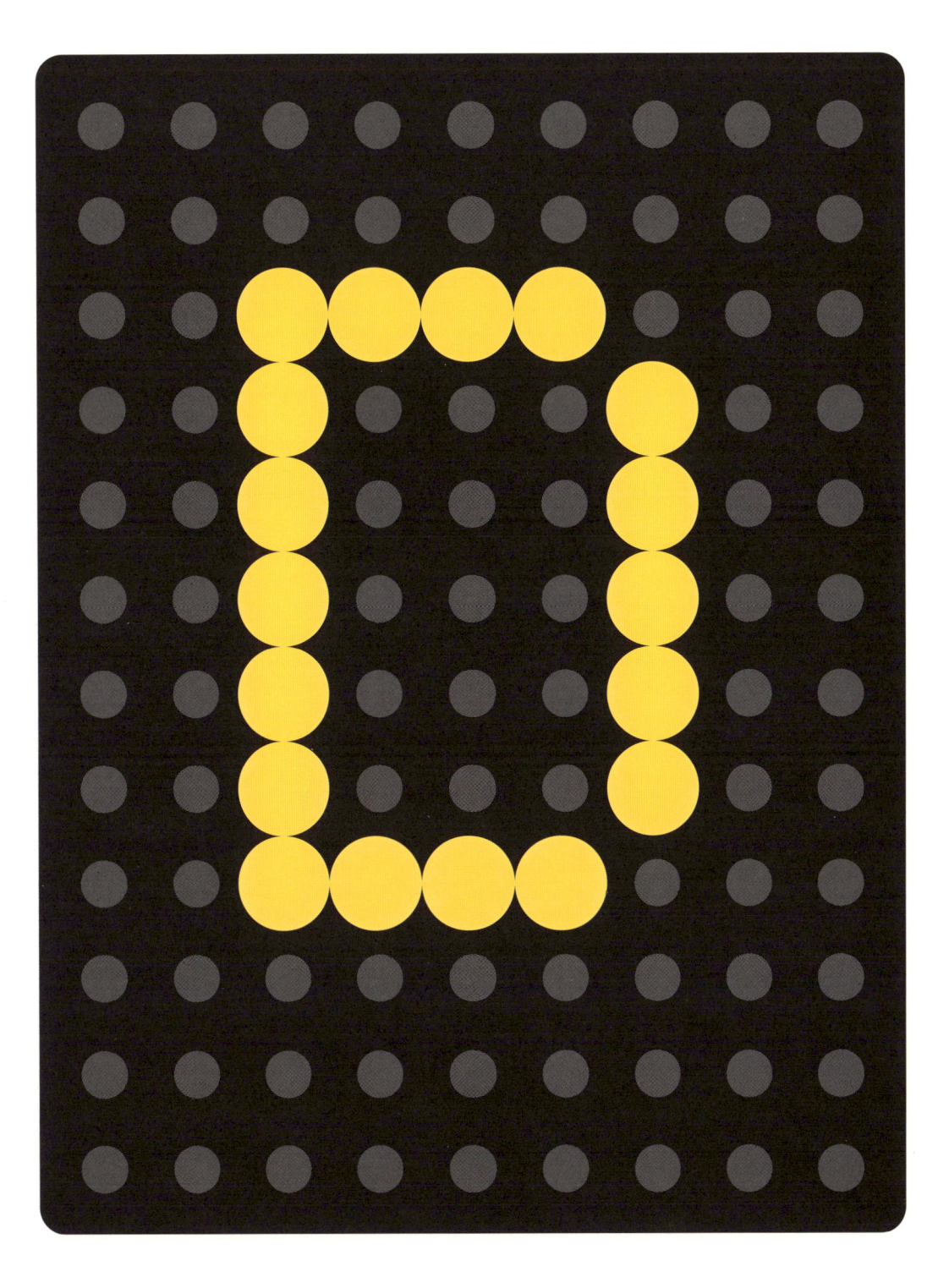

Digital
Angel Fernando Lara Moreira

In 1966 Cedric Price posed a conundrum: 'Technology is the answer, but what was the question?' This riddle is as relevant today as it was more than fifty years ago. John Frazer's 1968 project 'Flexible Enclosure System' (or the 'Reptile System'), perhaps the first architectural drawing generated by a computer program, was just the initial step in the digital revolution that has helped designers to explore new fields of aesthetics, information and production, with the digital model at its core.

Design through model-making is nothing new to architects and designers. The likes of Frei Otto and Antoni Gaudí became as celebrated for their numerous study models of form-finding, structure and material experimentation as for their specific architectural proposals. It is our desire for authenticity and sophistication in our design process that powers the digital as a comprehensive solution to overcome complex design problems through computer-aided design (CAD).

The current state of digital technologies allows us to model in three dimensions, enhance reality by creating new virtual environments, simulate physical forces, examine different material properties and analyse our architectural proposals through a variety of constraints and desired parameters. Design and drawing methods based on a traditional comprehension of geometry and space are today enhanced by data and algorithmic thinking, exponentially increasing our understanding of formal studies and their performance. Architects have a responsibility to explore different possible design solutions, as well as to understand, analyse and be critical of their spatial configuration, structural and environmental performance, urban considerations and material implications.

The digital grants us the means to generate an abundance of different proposals for defined projects and obtain almost immediate feedback. Data becomes a mechanism with which to test and simulate different conditions in our digital model. Solar exposure, radiance levels, shadow projection and façade surface temperatures can be understood in direct correlation to a proposed morphology, material or site constraint. Structural capabilities and performance become apparent from the early stages of design, and provide valuable insight into material and formal behaviour. This unprecedented access to data has allowed building information modelling (BIM) technologies to document and manage digitally all relevant information on a construction project across each of its stages. It allows for coherent cross-disciplinary collaboration to contribute to a single model that can be updated during both the design and build cycles. Likewise, new developments in rendering engines allow designers to test materials, views, textures and lighting

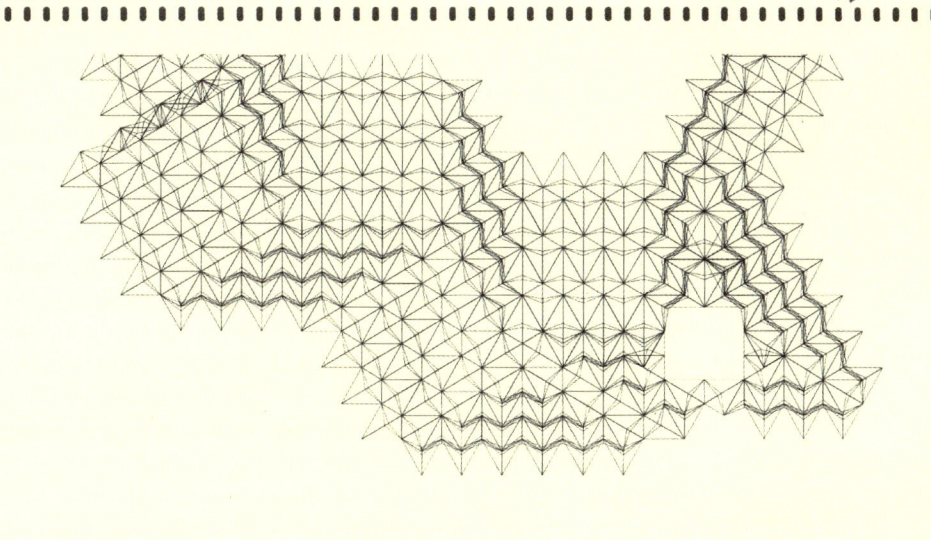

'Flexible Enclosure System' (1968) by John Frazer, in his fourth-year studio work at the Architectural Association, London.

conditions that are not readily available in a physical model. Exploring and understanding unbuilt architectural space through digital modelling is not only possible but standard practice to communicate design intentions.

Computational methods have challenged traditional modes of thinking and transformed the act of making through digital fabrication technologies. Computer numerical control (CNC) milling, robotic manufacturing and 3D printing and scanning have allowed digital models to be translated into built form, while reducing time and cost and providing a rapid succession of design and test models. The accuracy, material compatibility and speed of these methods translate into a design-and-make mode of production in which one iteration quickly leads to the next in a process as straightforward as modifying the underlying geometry and reuploading a new set of parameters or instructions. As digital tools become more accessible, the boundary between design office and construction site becomes less rigid, and prototyping becomes the standard pathway to a building. It all stems from the iterative nature of digital fabrication, in which a new model of design can express its full potential. The digital model can thus be conceived as an infinite resource. At its core it can be used to enter and extract information, to analyse (and it can itself be analysed), to synthesize and express an idea, and to advance its own manner of construction. It can encompass all stages of the design process, from concept and sketching through to built form; from structural analysis to spatial configurations and occupancy rates; and from 1:200 to 1:1 scale.

Perhaps the most important characteristic of our new digital tools is the way in which they have changed the process of design thinking, breaking away from the linearity of concept, proposal, model and building, towards a richer iterative mode in which the proposal can be tested, analysed, modified and redesigned as part of a more informed design process. The digital model's value lies in its ability to convert early-stage design ideas and data into tangible design proposals through this iterative process, providing a diversity of options before committing to a final solution. The digital model is now incorporated into every designer's workflow, and has allowed for experimentation through analysis, iteration, material and fabrication. As our built environment evolves and presents new challenges, so does our computational prowess. We might have forgotten the question, but digital technology has provided us with myriad tools and means of reply.

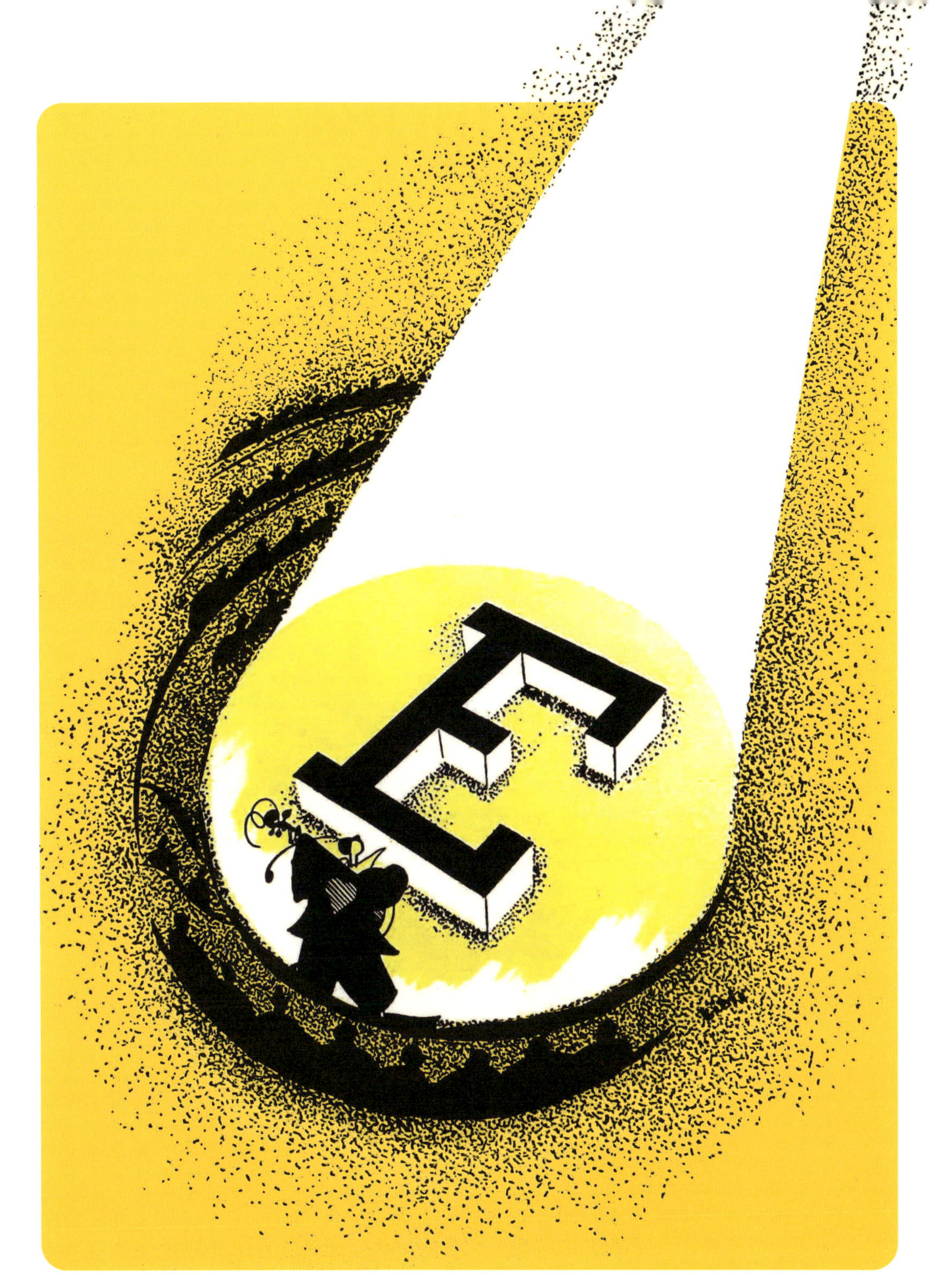

Exhibition
Spencer de Grey

Models play a significant role in the design and presentation of an architectural project. There is nothing new in this; Christopher Wren and John Soane built many models to develop and explain their designs. Models not only serve as a compelling way of testing and visualizing a project, but also they define a project, providing a sense of intent, of reality. They have always been integral to our design process. When I joined Foster Associates in 1973, the use of models was evident as both a design tool and a means of communication. People respond positively when they can see in miniature what a building looks like or how a space is going to feel. It no longer remains in the hazy realms of imagination, but jumps into life as a physical representation.

While models of finished buildings serve a defined purpose, they depict just the 'tip of the iceberg', with the bulk of the design process hidden beneath the surface. A typical project in our studio will generate many models as it progresses through an iterative design process. This helps us, our clients and other collaborators to understand the effect of a building on the urban realm and its own spatial qualities, both internal and external. We also use models to learn how the sun, wind and other climatic factors may affect building performance. By simulating airflow, using wind tunnels or employing 3D-printed models to see where structural stresses may occur, we can quickly evaluate the merits of a particular design. Detailed models facilitate decisions about materiality and textures, and enable engineers and fabricators to understand how a building will be put together in a way that a drawing cannot. We often model elements at life size to develop the design. For instance, we used Perspex, rainwater pipes and plastic grillage in 1980 to simulate the external wall of the HSBC Headquarters in Hong Kong; the model was extremely realistic and gave us a better idea of how the structure would look and feel in real life.

The steady growth of our in-house model-making team over the past few decades reflects the importance of the architectural model to our design process. The introduction of computers and computer-aided design in the mid-1980s has not reduced the need for models; it has increased it. There is no substitute for a physical representation. The process of design is a long journey, with abortive explorations and multiple revisions necessary to achieve the final result. We try to reveal this process through our exhibitions, which demystify the many hours of work that go into design. Buildings create the environment in which people live and work; this is what we endeavour to illustrate for an audience that often has little idea of an architect's work.

Over the last five decades, the practice has designed and participated in many exhibitions, those showcasing our own work, as well as others on specific themes and subjects. Technical drawings are likely to be unintelligible to everyone except those trained to work with them; it is akin to being able to read music. The simple combination of large photographs and self-explanatory models forms an extremely effective storytelling device, and has defined our approach to exhibition design.

In 2001, at the Louisiana Museum of Modern Art in Humlebæk, Denmark, we curated an exhibition called *The Architect's Studio*. It focused on two projects that shared an interest in ecology and responding to the natural context but were at opposite ends of the scale in terms of size, function and materiality: 30 St Mary Axe, an office tower in the heart of London, and Chesa Futura, a small apartment building perched on the mountainside above St Moritz, Switzerland. We explained each project through design development models, accompanied by a few hand sketches. The models illustrated the extensive research and design skills that we use to create buildings that are sustainable and built for a changing future.

Demystifying the design process through models has been an approach that the studio has followed since the early days. In the exhibition catalogue for *Foster Associates: Six Architectural Projects 1975–1985* at the Sainsbury Centre at the University of East Anglia in Norwich (1985), the Keeper, Derek Gillman, explained the simple 'didactic' purpose behind the exhibition: to give the public, which is 'frequently baffled by the processes of modern design and engineering ... the chance to see in

Large-scale display of models in the exhibition The Norman Foster Studio: Exploring the City *at the Sainsbury Centre, Norwich, 2000.*

some detail the way in which Foster Associates develop a project'. The models took centre stage, carefully demonstrating the key design principles that underpinned every project. Similarly, in 1986, a major exhibition called *New Architecture: Foster, Rogers, Stirling* was held at the Royal Academy of Arts in London, and positioned the work of these architects as representative of a new direction in British architecture. All three participants commissioned several large bespoke models that dramatically filled the galleries of the Royal Academy.

We have taken several divergent approaches to exhibition displays. We returned to the Sainsbury Centre in 2000 for an exhibition entitled *The Norman Foster Studio: Exploring the City*, where 100 models were set on a huge stepped platform signifying the city. Inspired by Joseph Michael Gandy's watercolour of 1818 depicting all of Sir John Soane's executed buildings in the form of theatrically lit models and presentation drawings, it was a dramatic display that both showcased the diversity of buildings and structures that exist in the city and communicated the breadth of work by the practice. By way of contrast, in 2006, in the exhibition *Norman Foster: Space and Time* within the grand spaces of the Pushkin State Museum of Fine Arts in Moscow, models were treated as artworks, carefully and beautifully crafted, individually presented and lit in the style of the museum, which prides itself on its globally important art collection.

More recently, as an architect Academician at the Royal Academy of Arts, I was invited to curate the Architecture Room for the 2019 Summer Exhibition, which celebrated sustainability within architecture in the broadest sense. Beneath a canopy of leaves of three silver birch trees, the models were envisaged as the centrepiece, displayed on stepped timber plinths and easy to understand and explore. The range of scales and the varied approaches throughout the works were striking; from 1:1 scale elements of a building to masterplan models made of sustainable materials, the objects served not just as a representation of an idea but also as an embodiment of the ideal of sustainability. The themes of each project's approach to a more sustainable world were identified through pithy captions – the first time that captions had been used for the Architecture Room.

Over the past twenty years, our models have toured worldwide, bringing our design thinking to audiences in more than thirty cities. Models are always at the heart of every exhibition, and several of them are historic artefacts themselves, dating back three decades or more. We increasingly use digital 3D models and virtual and augmented reality as tools to help clients visualize a building. This technology also influences how we conceptualize and plan our future exhibitions. The viewer is no longer seen as a passive recipient but as an active participant in the exhibition. Every year we open the doors of our London studios to the public for the Open House weekend; our visitors, especially the young children, enjoy the many models on display. The excitement and passion we put into our work are conveyed through our models in a way that other media cannot achieve. In successfully sharing these emotions lies the success of the exhibition.

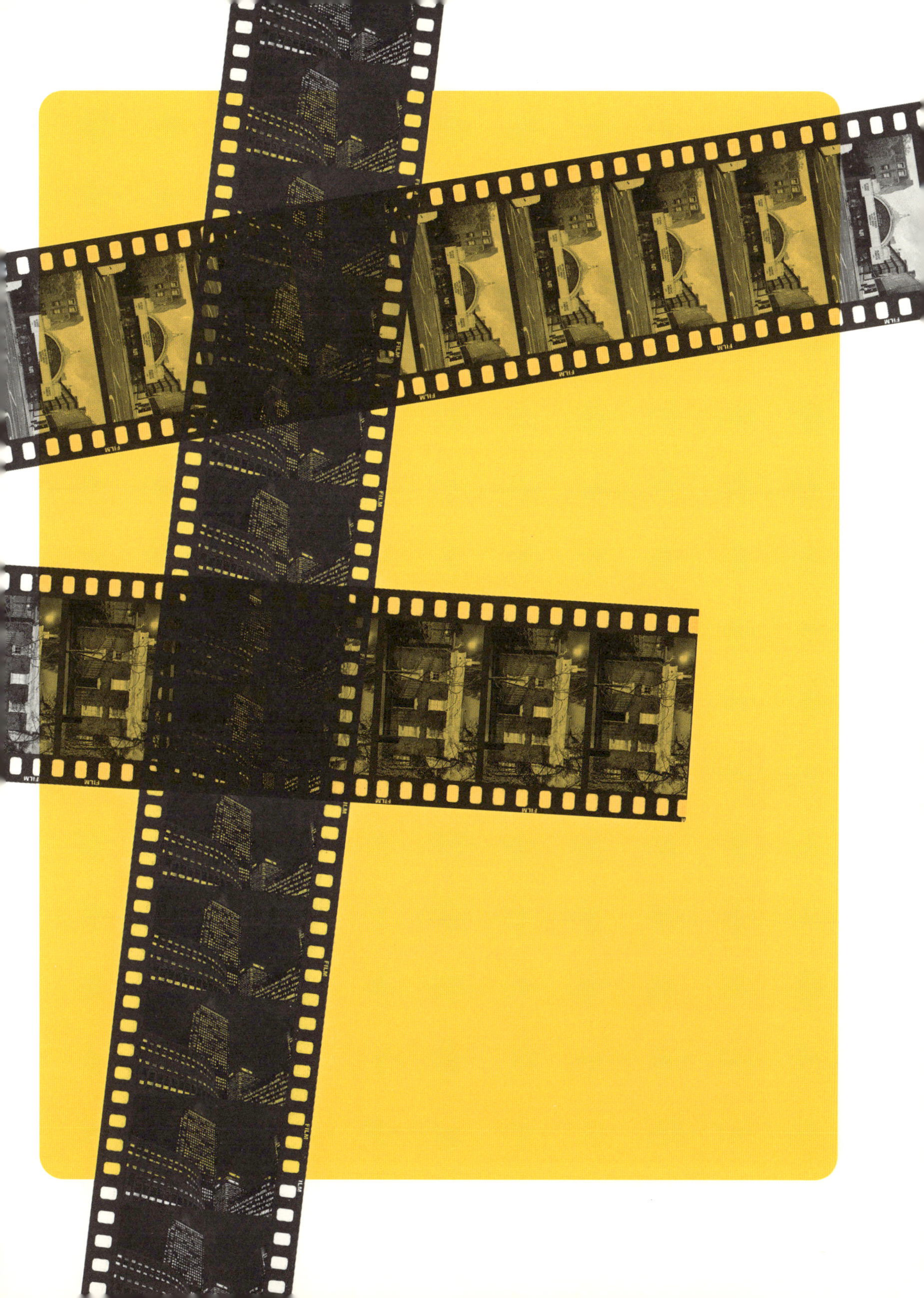
FILM

Film
Sarine Waltenspül

Filmic or cinematographic models can be found in films of almost all genres and periods. As a consequence of the unavailability of a full-size object (as in the case of spaceships, for example), the impossibility of destroying a subject (as in the demolition of the White House), or a director's personal interest or fetishism, models have been a part of cinema since its infancy. Contrary to common assumption, the emergence of computer-generated imagery (CGI) has led to only a limited decline in their use.

Because of this continuity, it is possible to ask what a history of film would look like if, instead of famous directors, costly blockbusters, ingenious technologies and grand theories, it focused on rather small, marginal and barely discernible objects such as scale models or miniatures. A history of cinema based on models reveals a very different story from that seen from traditional perspectives. The mere fact that miniatures are scaled objects locates them in a network of discourses, practices, techniques, epistemes and aesthetics that go far beyond the realm of the cinematic.

The intertwinement of the cinematographic with other fields that have traditionally worked with scale models is compellingly illustrated by two examples:

In the country-house thriller Hævnens nat *(English title:* Blind Justice; *DK 1916, Benjamin Christensen), an architectural model is used to introduce the most important protagonist: the house itself.*

fluid mechanics and architecture. In the 1920s, formulas developed in the field of fluid dynamics were transferred to film-technical discourse. Originally developed to convert measurements from model experiments to full scale, in film productions these formulas were used to calculate the correct recording frequency, and therefore helped to generate an impression of mass and size with scale models. This transfer of formulas was remarkable, as it showed the desire not only to create the 'perfect impression' of the real but also to enhance the entertainment-orientated potential of cinema with knowledge from fluid dynamics.

The desire to create an impression of mass and size with the miniature is also a topic in architecture. In architectural practice, photographs of models from the design process and in presentation contexts play a major role. Presentation models, in particular, are often photographed, not least because the images are easier to circulate than unwieldy models. Furthermore, photography allows the designer to create an impression of size by choosing the right viewpoint and by using backdrops rather than by standing a scale model on a table in an architect's office. Compared to photographs, moving images as film or video have played a less prominent role in architecture, but one not to be underestimated. As predigital films were complex and costly to produce, distribute and screen, it was only in exceptional cases that films of models were made for the presentation of architecture. One example is the 1939 National Socialist model film *Das Wort aus Stein* (The word in stone), directed by Kurt Rupli. In this *Kulturfilm*, realistically staged models simulated the Reich capital city, Germania (Hitler's proposed rebuilding of Berlin, under the direction of Albert Speer), in order to convince the population that the buildings were already, or would soon be, standing, so as to generate approval for the upcoming war. As Angela Schönberger claims in *Simulation und Wirklichkeit* (1988), it was this film and

In L'Écume des jours *(English title:* Mood Indigo; *F/B 2013, Michel Gondry), adapted from the eponymous novel by Boris Vian, Gondry realizes Vian's surreal world through the conspicuous use of models.*

photographs of the models that, in the aftermath of the Second World War, led to negative connotations associated with the concept of simulation. Films of models were also produced in other totalitarian states at this time. The interplay of scale models and specific recording techniques influenced not only contemporary but also future film audiences, as the distrust in simulations shows. In this instance, models were of political significance and made a cultural impact beyond the confines of architecture and film.

In film history, the connections between cinematography and other, primarily non-visual fields, such as fluid dynamics, are under-represented. Therefore, the consideration of scale models as 'crossover' objects alongside corresponding film techniques can help to bridge disciplinary boundaries. It can also serve to broaden the realm of the cinematographic beyond a focus on authors to include objects, materiality, knowledge, discourse and the practice-based history of film.

This is important, because cinematographic models still shape contemporary cinema, from blockbusters to art-house films. The fascination for the miniature and the desire for seduction that comes with its cinematic enlargement are synchronous and also increasingly interwoven. Again, this can be read as paradigmatic for the simultaneously monstrous and shrunken world in which we live today. In refocusing from the big to the small, film and cinema show themselves as a network of relationships, as an open system whose techniques and aesthetics move between areas and disciplines, and are implemented, adapted and absorbed again. The potential of models can hardly be overestimated.

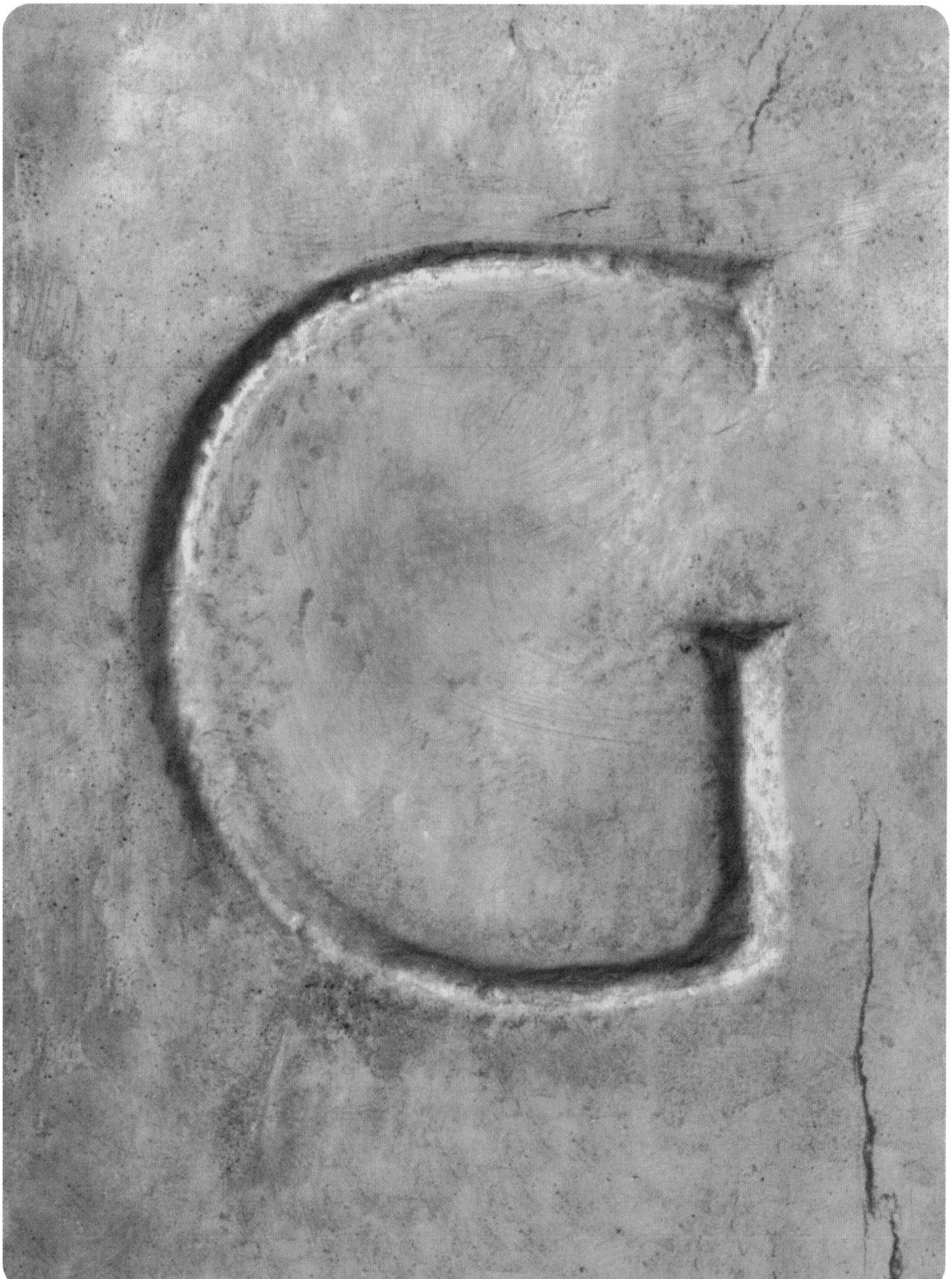
G

Gypsum
Mari Lending

The Greek word γύψος (*gypsos*) appears in English as *gypsum*, and in Norwegian and German as *Gips*. In the world of mineralogy, this sulfate mineral composed of calcium sulfate dihydrate has the chemical formula $CaSO_4 \cdot 2H_2O$, and it constituted the plaster/*plâtre* mixtures used for many years in various kinds of architectural models. Its French reference has remained strong; in English, gypsum is still often called 'plaster of Paris' on account of the quarries in Montmartre that provided burned, or calcined, gypsum to the worlds of art and architecture.

Models reveal aspects of architecture that are unavailable in the reality of the built world. The power of this revelation is beautifully captured in Stendhal's *Mémoires d'un touriste* (1838), a novel disguised as a travelogue. In Nimes, the traveller visits the amphitheatre, the Maison Carrée, the Augustus Gate and the ancient baths, before setting out for the Pont du Gard on his way to Orange. However, the experience of seeing the awe-inspiring ancient Roman ruins at first hand is rendered empty by the experience of the miniature versions of the same monuments: 'One could not see a more skilful or exact imitation. These models, all executed on the same scale, enabled me to have an idea of the comparative size of those monuments for the first time.' Stendhal – the pseudonym of Marie-Henri Beyle, or his alter ego in this book, 'M.L.' – had seen the French architect and archaeologist Auguste Pelet's collection of 1:100 scale cork models of Roman monuments, which were later catalogued in their maker's posthumously published *Description des monuments grecs et romains exécutés en liège à l'échelle d'un centimètre par mètre* (Nîmes, 1876). In Stendhal's fictitious memoir, Pelet's verisimilar collection demonstrates how the miniature enables a more accurate understanding of buildings, and also highlights the way in which the comparative effects of models might radically alter the perception of what is seen and experienced beyond mere representation. Stendhal corroborates a common experience of architecture *in situ* – namely, the feeling of a building being lost in context, of surprise and disappointment in the discovery that famous buildings often tend to be much smaller than expected. In their abstracted simplicity, removed from the distractions of reality, models reveal proportions, space and scale, leading Stendhal's traveller to the surprising realization that 'the Arch of Triumph at Orange, a gigantic work, would easily pass under one of the lower arches of the Pont du Gard'.

Plaster models at full scale have a different claim to reality, representing size rather than scale. In 1876, for the inauguration of the *Cour vitrée* at the École des Beaux-Arts in Paris, two enormous casts were placed in the glass-covered courtyard of the Palais des Études. The collaborative work of three Prix de Rome recipients and

The cast of Trajan's Column under construction in the West Court of the Architectural Courts at the South Kensington Museum, London, photographed by Isabel Agnes Cowper in 1873.

two of the world's finest moulders ensured that the north-western corner of the Parthenon and a hyper-styled, restored version of the Temple of Castor and Pollux colonnade in the Roman Forum could serve as gypsum models for students in their *dimensions réelles*. Three years earlier, reporting from the recently inaugurated Architectural Courts at the South Kensington Museum (now the Victoria and Albert Museum) in London, an anonymous reviewer for *The Builder* magazine compared the experience of entering the sky-lit galleries to 'the first entrance to Notre Dame, Paris; the first glimpse of Mont Blanc'. Mesmerized by the properties of the space and the massiveness of the plaster monuments, the reviewer found Trajan's Column the most remarkable reproduction, and claimed that it bestowed 'advantages not enjoyed in Rome'. The life-sized models were perceived and discussed as architecture, but also as something more. The London version of Trajan's Column provided a better perceptual experience than the original monument in Rome;

the column's immense size was even more apparent when the monument was decontextualized and domesticated in a museum.

An unforgettable portrayal of the relation between a perfect model and a ruined building is found in a novel written and published as the tide was turning against the plaster cast as a mass medium. Marcel Proust, however, did not share his contemporaries' increasing distaste for plaster: his thinking on the value of reproductions fundamentally challenges his German translator Walter Benjamin's notion of 'aura' as being a quality integral to an artwork. In *In Search of Lost Time* (1913–27), a work of art's irreducible particularity does not reside in its material authenticity. One of the first and most compelling objects of desire introduced in Proust's novel is a medieval church portal exhibited at the Musée de Sculpture Comparée in Paris, which – today as the Musée des Monuments Français – is among the finest collections of plaster casts in the world. Finally in front of the real church in the fictitious town of Balbec in Normandy, in a long-awaited moment, the protagonist-narrator unexpectedly finds himself desperately longing to return to the museum in Paris. He finds the church trivialized by its surroundings, by such prosaic elements as a square, a café, a billiard saloon, a bank, a bus station, street lamps and trams. Marcel expected 'the church itself, the statue in person, the real things!' to be more imposing than their plaster doubles in Paris, but they turn out to be 'much less'. Reduced to 'nothing but its own shape in stone', the portal is, as Proust sensationally puts it, caught in 'the tyranny of the Particular'. While the model in the gallery appeared universal and immortal, 'endowed with a general existence and an inaccessible beauty', the portal *in situ* is lost in context, the victim of time and reality.

H

Hand
Oliver Elser

On a tenth-century mosaic in the Hagia Sophia in Istanbul, two models are depicted. One shows the Hagia Sophia itself with a vague similarity to the real building (which was constructed as the cathedral for the capital of the Eastern Roman Empire), the other is a rather cartoonish model of the city of Constantinople, as Istanbul was formerly known. Both models are in the hands of emperors, who seem to present them to the Virgin Mary, seated in the middle of the mosaic with the infant Christ on her lap. In the history of the architectural model, pictures or sculptures of donors, or of otherwise supportive figures, are the very first traces of the various ways in which the human hand is able to present, dominate, create or dismantle a miniature. These donors' models could inspire a debate on another subject – namely, if they are realistic representations of the churches, or if their shapes are purely symbolic abstraction. But one aspect is undeniable: the gesture of the hands is devotional. The model, whether accurate or not, is handed over from one person to another.

In a photograph from 1985, the real estate businessman Donald Trump's hand touches a model of a skyscraper in a completely different way. His fat fingers seem to squeeze the slick tower, which resembles the Empire State Building but is in fact the centrepiece of the proposed Television City project on the Upper West Side of Manhattan by Helmut Jahn. The hand on the model in the age of photography is a marker for our eyes. Whenever a hand appears, it leads to the interpretation that a powerful person wants us to see the model as a functional tool. Devotion turns into possession. The hand no longer 'hands over' the model. Holding a model shifts from 'giving' to 'explaining', which in many cases is connected to a gesture of domination.

Explanatory hands can be found in art as early as the sixteenth century, in a Renaissance painting (in the Palazzo Vecchio) that depicts Cosimo de' Medici pointing with one hand to a model and with the other to the construction site of the basilica of San Lorenzo in Florence: *this*, the model, will soon be *that*, the real building. In the famous 'wine-rack' photograph of about 1946, the hand of Le Corbusier plugs a module of an apartment into a model of the structural frame of his Unité d'Habitation in Marseilles to explain his ideas on prefabricated housing. The scene could be from a short film or a stage performance: empty skeleton + housing modules = finished building. End of play. In the works of OMA or MVRDV, numerous images of models – often series of photographs – show a hand, occasionally an arm or a full body, that explains the design by cutting and folding sheets of paper. In a video presentation from 2009 of his 8 House project in Copenhagen, Bjarke Ingels turns this into a whole bodily performance, transforming

Ludwig Mies van der Rohe in June 1954, presenting the model for Crown Hall on the Illinois Institute of Technology campus, before the project was finally approved in September of that year.

a virtual model in his real office. In these examples, the hand is that of the demiurge, a godlike being, who acts as a giant, forming first the small things, later the larger reality. The well-known *Time* magazine cover of January 1979 with Philip Johnson holding a model of the AT&T Building in New York as a trophy adds to these tropes of the architect as a divine figure: the preacher of Postmodernism as a Moses lookalike, presenting his design instead of the Ten Commandments.

It might not be a coincidence that the interplay of two women is needed to break this scheme. In a photograph of Kazuyo Sejima taken by Annie Leibovitz in 2006 for *Vogue* magazine, the architect lies in the dunes, holding a model of her New Museum in New York in her hand as if she has just found this strange object on the beach. The Japanese architect shows no sign of domination; rather, she is simply curious, and holds her own model with an expression of astonishment.

By way of contrast, the most male gesture is made by Helmut Jahn, who, in a photograph of 1996 by Abe Frajndlich for *Der Spiegel* magazine, clasps a model in a way that says, 'This is all mine.' Dominant actions are multifarious in Ludwig Mies van der Rohe's interactions with models as well. His heavy hand rests on a bronze model of the Seagram Building in New York, seen by photographer Irving Penn in 1955. Or, in 1954, he seems to test the stability of the trusses of his Crown Hall in Chicago, but in a sensitive way. Yet Mies would never have put his feet on an architectural model. That happened only in a photo shoot for the first design of the Seagram skyscraper, when the company's president, Victor A. Fischel, wanted to subordinate the model for the sake of his own greatness. Phyllis Lambert, the daughter of Seagram's owner, became involved in the project shortly after this episode, and established Mies as the architect with an austere design that only Mies himself was allowed to touch.

Mies van der Rohe is perhaps the architect most frequently photographed alongside architectural models. He posed in numerous positions: looking at models, touching them, pointing at them with a sharp pencil, discussing millimetres of architectural expression with his employees. Before he became a photographic subject, a pencil cartoon from about 1925 by his assistant Sergius Ruegenberg shows Mies crouching down, turning a model of a glass skyscraper in his hands to examine the reflections on the curved glass façades. In this drawing, the hand is in its most natural position: handling a working model. For any other architect, this would not have been a big deal. Adjusting a working model, trying this or that, is the most common of practices. Not for Mies. He had never before used curvilinear plans, which, he noted in 1922 in the periodical *Frühlicht*, 'appeared at first glance … arbitrary', but were instead 'the result of many experiments using a glass model'. Never again would Mies return to architecture as a result of an interaction between his hands, eyes, glass and light.

For Mies's contemporary Wassili Luckhardt the use of the hands in the design process was not common at all. A hand holding a pencil, yes, of course. But that meant, for Luckhardt, that the brain already knew what to draw. He wanted to omit this sketching stage: 'Put pencil and paper aside, take clay or plasticine and begin modelling, from scratch, directly and without influence', he wrote in the journal *Stadtbaukunst alter und neuer Zeit* in 1921. The use of a working model was rare in those days.

Shortly afterwards, such Expressionist architects as Carl Krayl and Hans Poelzig started crafting models from plaster and clay with their hands. There is an anecdote about the Late Expressionist Gottfried Böhm that is apocryphal but nevertheless too good to be left out: in the second competition in 1964 for the Pilgrimage Church of Neviges, North Rhine-Westphalia, the architect presented a plasticine model made with his own hands. The design for the mountain-like church might have been considered too idiosyncratic to be presented in any other way than the artistic medium of the *bozzetto*, a small rough clay study for a larger sculpture, used since the time of the Renaissance. According to the story, the nearly blind Archbishop of Cologne, Josef Frings, felt the model with his hands before giving his approval for Böhm's design. The hands of the two men connected through the medium of the plasticine model. And so perception and creation came about through sensitive modelling and examination by hand.

We know of barely any images of architects that show them simply playing with a working model, be it in plasticine, paper or any other material. Maybe this would seem too childish, even though it happens every day. The pictures we know are mostly propaganda, carefully curated to portray a certain kind of serious attitude on the part of the architect towards the model and the world.

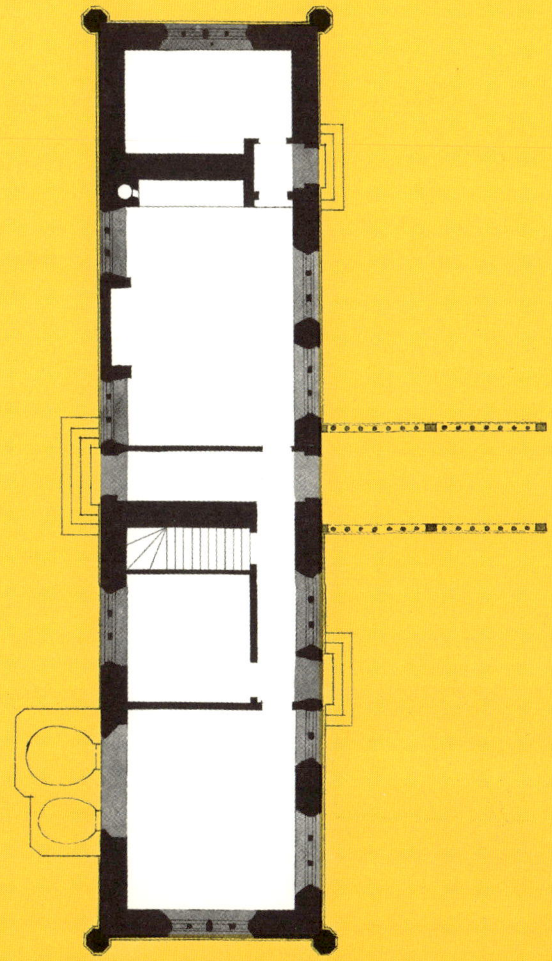

Inspiration
Roz Barr

The act of making involves engaging with an idea that can be made, unmade and reconsidered before being realized. For me, the process of working through the evolution of an idea is best explored through model-making. This form of making is about the discourse of architectural thinking, and it has a critical role in formulating and realizing an idea. We imagine, we make, and our ideas, such as those about materiality and form, develop through discussions while we construct the maquette. Nothing is fixed in this process; our ideas are continually evolving as we transfer them into physical form.

Each model embodies a moment in a design stage and acts as a catalyst for future phases of the architectural process. A model crystallizes ideas and sometimes provokes immediate realizations about scale or placement on a site. It is in the act of making, whether carving blocks of wood or creating the mould for a plaster cast, that we have time to allow an idea to evolve. Model-making can be seen as ritualistic, for it produces a material form that through physical engagement allows for a meaningful intervention. This aspect is possibly what I find most engaging about it as a process for designing and making.

Initial thoughts for projects or sites are instinctual, driven by their context, the parameters of the brief and the content to be contained. First ideas are sketched by hand, but the need to transpose them into a three-dimensional maquette follows

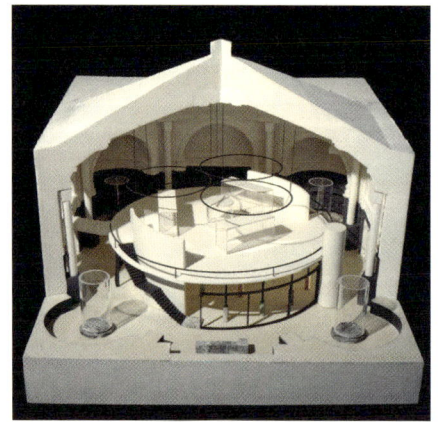

Concept model at 1:75 scale in cast plaster from Roz Barr Architects' winning competition entry in 2019 for the Fashion Gallery at the Victoria and Albert Museum, London.

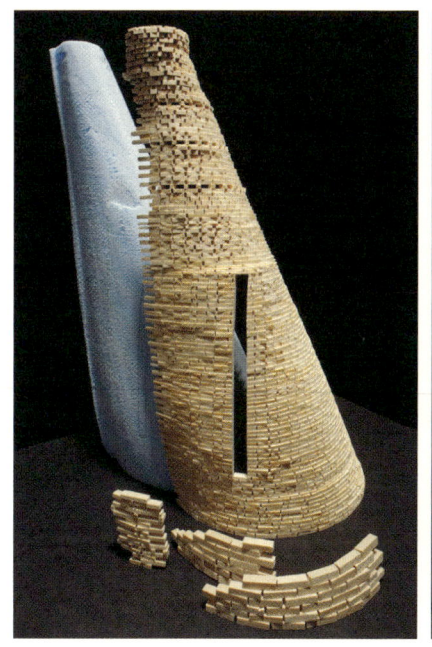

In their 2012 competition entry for the church in Valer, Norway, plywood blocks stacked around a polystyrene form allowed Roz Barr Architects to test their proposal for the dome's interior.

very quickly. Sketching and drawing continue in tandem with this process, and allow the maquette to be driven by considerations of scale and materiality. When I established the studio, there were restrictions on our ability to make models. We had desk space within the office of a large engineering company, and there was no model-making facility. We either developed ideas at our desks or set up a place to make at meeting tables once everyone else had left for the day. It did not deter us, and during this time, in 2012, we made a beautiful timber model for the competition for the church in Valer, Norway.

The idea for the form of this new church was conceived as a watercolour-paper maquette, which evolved from a site model that we carved from a piece of lemonwood. The concept for the conical dome of the church was engineered to allow solid timber blocks to be stacked within the shroud of a shuttered timber external façade. I knew that if we could develop the model at a larger scale, we could test the premise of its construction and also create a form that could be photographed as part of the submission. We tested ideas for the form of the church through smaller maquettes; we knew that the concept worked, and so over a long weekend we built the model on a conference-room table while we drew and completed the submission boards. This model defined the possibilities of 'craft' within the physical manipulation of a single material – plywood stacked around a formwork that we had machine-tooled in polystyrene. Through the stacking of the miniature plywood blocks, the storytelling and narrative of the project became embedded in the design process. Although we did not win the international competition (we were awarded joint second place), this project confirmed my intuition that an idea's strength is developed through the physical transformation of making the maquette.

The inspiration for maquettes is often born from the materials with which we work. This was very much a factor in the search for our first studio in London. I wanted a workshop, a place in which to make and experiment. We invested in a table saw, a wood sander and other equipment, and we made our own workbenches. We subsequently moved, and now our model-making area is within the same space as our design studio. Although we cannot make as much mess, it does not hinder the creative process.

Casting in plaster is, I think, the most rewarding model-making process. There is something ritualistic and measured about it that allows ideas to develop and be adapted. It requires drawing and understanding the parameters of an idea, and you can test several ideas with one pour. There is also something intensely satisfying about breaking the formwork and discovering the results within. Cast plaster produces effects that allow for creative ambiguity, and the imperfections can prompt quick decisions about whether to continue or to stop. Our first cast models for a tower house in Scotland (2016) were studies on fenestration and stone coursing. These development models were part of a family of maquettes that explored ideas, and proved to be a quick way of working – almost physical sketches.

In 2019 we constructed a large, complex plaster model as part of our submission for the competition to design the new Fashion Gallery at the Victoria and Albert Museum in London. It was a sectional model through Aston Webb's Octagonal Court. I wanted to show the purity of the existing volume, which had been severed by the construction of a mezzanine in the 1960s. The energy in the studio as we made and imagined was very special, and our success in winning the competition was embedded in realizing our ideas through the process of making this physical proposal.

Maquettes and models are more widely used in architecture to show a site within the context of a city or landscape. While such models are important, I also very much enjoy realizing an idea at a larger scale, and as a studio we have built full-size installations that are maquettes to be inhabited, such as the Tin Chapel at St Augustine's Church in Hammersmith, west London (2018).

We built a range of scale models for our work at St Augustine's. We made that of the Cast-Iron Tower (2017), an extension to the Community Centre dating from the 1960s, in tulipwood at a scale of 1:10. This model of a proposed 20-metre-tall (65½ ft) tower was used in the consultation process and for an exhibition that allowed the priests and community to understand the quality of spaces internally and the rhythm and detail of the façades. From large building elements of the project to designs for smaller items of liturgical furniture, models were a crucial part of the design process. The family of models and studies demonstrates the richness of three-dimensional thought that underpins the success of this body of work.

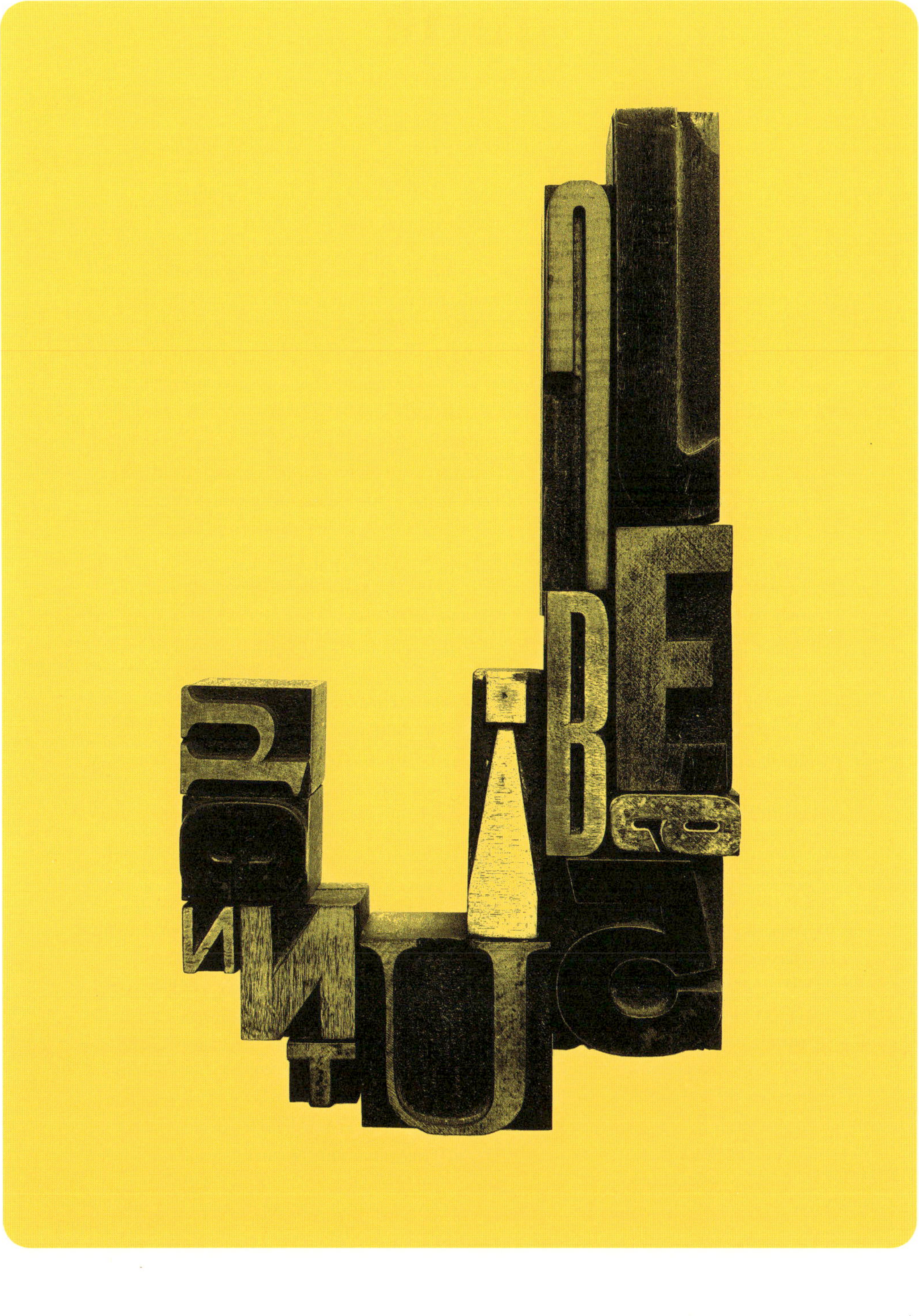

Junk
Martin Hartung

Around 1967, Arnold Behr photographed a pile of discarded planning models that the British architect Denys Lasdun and his team had used in the – evidently intense – design process for the National Theatre in London. On the occasion of his appointment as a Royal Academician in 1991, the architect added to the depicted 'model dump' a drawing of his own right hand sketching the completed complex. The well-known photograph was taken in Lasdun's studio at 50 Queen Anne Street in the West End of London. It was subsequently titled *Models in Dialogue* in a monograph on Lasdun's architecture office published by the Royal Institute of British Architects (RIBA) in 1976, the same year in which the famous Brutalist building was inaugurated. On the one hand, the photograph illustrates the architectural model as design tool, employed to foresee a variety of challenging issues associated with a building project and discarded when no longer needed. The impressive number of architectural models used in this instance refers to what Lasdun called the complex's 'very troubled passage'. On the other hand, the photograph alludes to the ambiguous status of the built model as an object in its own right.

By the time construction of the theatre started in 1969, the depicted models had long outlived their usefulness, but had they been 'wasted'? Were they junk? It depends on the point of view, as the urban planner Kevin Lynch outlines in his thoughtful survey *Wasting Away* (1990). He recognizes that 'any loss ... due to normal wear under adequate maintenance ... is not waste, but expected cost'. Lynch elaborates that 'abandonment makes waste ... [It] can be painful when it is involuntary. In other cases, it may be a liberation.' Aside from 'adequate maintenance', which is highly questionable considering their trashed state in the picture, the fact that the models were ultimately abandoned does not defy the basic realization that 'nothing is inherently trash', as the historian Susan Strasser phrases it in *Waste and Want* (1999), an influential study of the role and levels of waste in Western societies. In the mid-1960s, the anthropologist Mary Douglas assessed that 'dirt is relative', which, in Strasser's words, leads to 'systematic ordering and classifying'. The historian indicates the relationship between 'the toolbox and the junk box', made productive by the figure of the inventive *bricoleur*, whom Claude Lévi-Strauss introduced in *The Savage Mind* (1962). Lévi-Strauss ties the *bricoleur* to 'small-scale models' or 'miniatures'. In all of them, he assumes an 'intrinsic aesthetic quality'.

According to Lynch, the word 'junk' was once used for 'old but reusable iron, glass, and paper [but] is now a general term for any useless, broken-up, nonfunctioning thing'. The example of Lasdun not only points to the fact that loss is a recurring theme in the history of architectural models, it also refers to their ambivalent object status; the model is not just a tool, but, as Karen Moon comments in her book *Modeling Messages* (2005), 'also has an independent existence as an object, quite apart from the project with which it is associated'. This observation is consistent with the position of the architect Peter Eisenman, who prominently advocated the model's autonomy 'as the conceptual reality of architecture' in the context of the exhibition *Idea as Model*, which opened at the Institute for Architecture and Urban Studies in New York in 1976. Eisenman aimed to show 'that models, like architectural drawings, could well have an artistic or conceptual existence of their own'. Counter to this hermetic approach, the artist Gordon Matta-Clark – whose contribution to the exhibition was rejected by Eisenman at short notice – had in 1970 realized a community-oriented *Garbage Wall* as social commentary. Two years later, he organized a special arrangement of construction debris in a dumpster for an open-air exhibition in Lower Manhattan titled *Open House*. Ultimately, *Idea as Model* was not considered a success, partly because a number of contributions had already been realized elsewhere; Robert A.M. Stern, for example, simply directed a staff member to 'dust off' his existing model of a New York town-house façade.

Between the staging of the exhibition and the subsequent publication of the catalogue in 1981, new values had been assigned to architectural representations and records. A heightened public interest in the built environment was mirrored by the foundation of architecture museums and study centres in the 1970s, after a period of concentrated academic debates in the 1960s and a range of activities associated with architectural preservation, largely in response to Post-War Modernism. The attention paid to previously discarded materials informed a specialized market for architectural representations that developed at a time of scarce commissions. Primarily focused on architectural drawings, it also included models offered for sale by private individuals and art galleries. A prominent example was the New York-based Max Protetch Gallery, which became

Photograph of room with models, with added perspective drawing by Denys Lasdun of the National Theatre, South Bank, London, 1991.

the leading venue in this sector. The gallery's first solo exhibition with an architect – Michael Graves – in the spring of 1979, included numerous models from his studio. Despite such unusual attention being given to architectural models, they still accounted for less than 10 per cent of all the exhibits. Two façade models were sold, and the exhibition as a whole was an unprecedented monetary success. Furthermore, as James Wines from the studio SITE recalled, it was common practice to be asked to gift models as part of an institutional acquisition. Even though Heinrich Klotz, the founding Director of the Deutsches Architekturmuseum (DAM) in Frankfurt am Main and a prominent 'motor' of this short-lived market, emphasized the importance of collecting architectural models along with other comprehensive materials, the art market instead reflected an assessment that John Harris made as Curator of the RIBA Heinz Gallery during the first conference of the International Confederation of Architectural Museums in Helsinki in 1979. There, he described the discrepancy between the urge to collect as much material as possible, including architects' papers, and the limitations of the individual institution. With the Heinz Gallery in mind and probably confirming Klotz's ambitions, he stated that, in light of spatial constraints, 'We despair of saving architectural models, but after all, models very often tell you more than a drawing and are, from the public point of view, more alluring and comprehensible.'

After the DAM was founded in 1979, Klotz repeatedly recalled one of the main reasons for establishing an architecture museum: the inability to rescue a model of Ludwig Mies van der Rohe's last project, the Toronto-Dominion Centre, which had 'found its way onto the rubbish heap'. Noticing 'how hardly a single original model by a contemporary [international] architect ... had survived' up until that point in time, Klotz decided to build a collection. When he was finally equipped with funds, he pursued a special interest in models; today the DAM houses one of the world's largest model collections, with more than 1300 objects. In his most intense period of acquisition, between 1980 and 1982, Klotz was able to rescue the model of the Piazza d'Italia in New Orleans directly from the dumpster, where it had been discarded by August Perez & Associates, who cooperated on the design with Charles Moore. The office later tried to buy the model back and made a substantial offer, but Klotz refused. Despite this success, 'Robert Venturi [in turn] admitted that he had thrown out all his [models], keeping nothing.' In several instances, depending on the value assigned to the related projects, Klotz was eventually able to commission the reconstruction of models that were lost. Lasdun, however, maintained that models are 'a means of visualizing rather than a finished object to be gloated over in a glass case'.

The decision to retain and appreciate a three-dimensional architectural model or to abandon it was not only related to the urge to preserve historical evidence threatened by the fragility of common construction materials, but also remained closely tied to the issue of autonomy. When the market began to slow down in the late 1980s, mainly because of a shift of focus by architecture offices in light of global building commissions and the increased use of computerized planning tools, an entirely new set of challenges emerged, culminating in the museological twin tasks of preserving physical objects and saving data from the digital 'rubbish heap'.

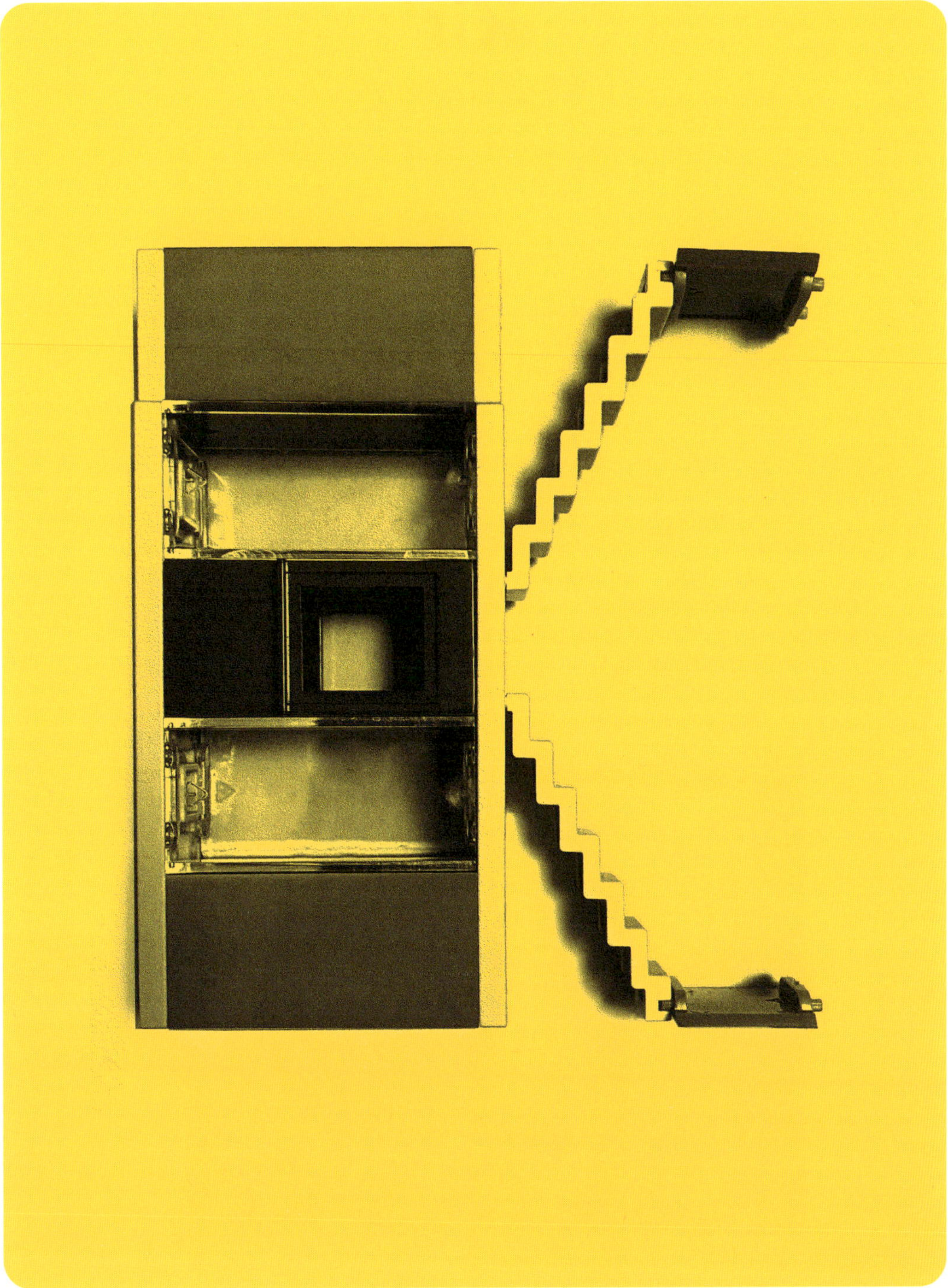

Kit
Vanessa Norwood

Kit. The word conjures up a travelling salesman moving from town to town, suitcase in hand. The infamous architect with a book of buildings ready to sell; a town hall here, an art gallery there – a kit of parts waiting to be built. 'Kit' makes it sound easy; nothing to suggest the deliberation, the slow, thoughtful design process or the specificity of site. Just pick something from the suitcase.

The word belongs to the realm of childhood; Lego, Meccano and Stickle Bricks assembled into swaying towers and unsteady bridges, ready to be demolished by unscrupulous four-year-old town planners.

Wooden building blocks have enthralled children for around two centuries. The German educator Friedrich Fröbel coined the word 'kindergarten' in the nineteenth century, and went on to revolutionize play with his design of a kit known as 'Fröbel's Gifts'. The kit contained geometric building blocks that are said to have influenced architects and artists alike. In the United States in 1913, the educational reformer Caroline Pratt took inspiration from Fröbel to create unit blocks, wooden bricks of different shapes and sizes that have encouraged generations of children to think modular, using the blocks as tools with which to explore the social and physical world around them.

Representation of Tadao Ando's Church of the Light in Ibaraki, Osaka, Japan (1989), rendered in Arckit components by Damien Murtagh, founder of Arckit.

Devotees of Frank Hornby's eponymous brand of miniature trains span all age groups. Hornby presents a world of ready-mades to populate a village landscape at a scale of 1:76; it is a kit that evokes the 1920s England of its creation, complete with fish and chip shops, cricket pavilions and village pubs. Hornby's first foray into kits had come twenty years earlier, when he devised Meccano, a model construction kit intended to teach children the basics of mechanics. Meccano enabled generations of both children and adults to make working models from metal strips, gears and wheels.

The appeal of the architectural model can be traced back to our childhood sense of awe at seeing the world miniaturized. A quick trawl of the internet will reveal that the market for architectural kits is booming. It is possible to buy a kit for a miniature Dutch farmhouse with a resin roof and ceramic walls, or, for those with more time on their hands, there is a matchstick modelling kit of St Paul's Cathedral. Companies such as Arckit aim their architectural modelling system at kids, students and architects alike, with the explicit ambition to 'open up the world of architecture to everyone'.

Kits make designers of us all. The ability to create townscapes in hours is a compelling challenge. The kit and its component parts create a connection to the process of building – a fixing-together with our hands.

The scale of a kit can vary from toy to supersize. Kit architecture at a scale of 1:1 retains the magic of its scaled-down counterparts. First exhibited in Oslo in 2006, dRMM's Naked House is a flat-pack kit designed to be built on top of the container in which the component parts were shipped. Naked House has the feel of a toy house on a massive scale, complete with a cut-out of a human figure. The idea of the house was that it could be dismantled, repacked and re-erected on a new site. It functions

Scale model of dRMM's Naked House (2006), a 1:1 kit described as 'a modest manifesto for personalized prefabricated timber architecture'.

as a supersized cut-out diagram with elements numbered for construction, including door and window openings, all digitally pre-cut from substantial cross-laminated timber panels.

The kit provides a way of understanding the built environment piece by piece. In the 1970s Walter Segal popularized the self-build movement. Segal's method proposed an architecture of components – a kit consisting of trusses, walls and beams – that enabled anyone with the most rudimentary knowledge of tools to build their own house through the acquisition of skills. Design was demystified, and architecture became a democratic pursuit. Segal used a Perspex model with moveable parts to help families create the best layout for their needs.

The first post-and-beam Huf Haus appeared in 1972; a sophisticated, customizable kit of parts using wood and glass as its building materials. More recently, WikiHouse, an open-source technology providing a digitally manufactured building system, aims to make it simple for anyone to design, manufacture and assemble their own home. Hawkins\Brown used WikiHouse's flexible form to great effect at Here East for its transformation of the former Broadcast Centre in the Queen Elizabeth Olympic Park in London. The spatial and structural constraints of the building's exterior gantry made the flat-packed modules the perfect choice as they could be assembled on site.

The conversation about the benefits of kit housing and larger-scale off-site construction is gaining momentum. A kit of factory-made components delivered to site ready to install offers distinct advantages over on-site construction, with its lengthy disruption and noise. Alongside retrofitting, the idea that, having reached the end of their lives, buildings can be dismantled and repurposed through the remanufacturing and recycling of materials is becoming increasingly urgent.

The kit is being developed further through new technologies. Block Type A, created by the Bartlett School of Architecture's Automated Architecture (AUAR) Labs, explores radical new ideas of automating the ways in which we build. It uses robots to construct houses, disassemble them and rebuild them again in different contexts. Block Type A addresses the high cost of land and property and our inefficient use of domestic space by proposing a system that allows us to share both space and belongings according to need. It could be described as a kit to rationalize our kit.

The kit's capacity for speedy construction was exploited by Extinction Rebellion during protests in London in October 2019. The protesters made use of easy-to-assemble wooden blocks adapted from Studio Bark's U-Build system, and cut-outs enabled them to chain themselves to the modular structure once it was built. The kit transformed into an architecture of protest; a literal and metaphorical platform for action.

The kit provides a process that, with component parts, can enable the democratization of architecture. A sibling to the architectural model, the kit is both a system with rules and instructions and a collection of pieces. The opportunities to shape space are endless.

L

Landscape
Isabelle Warmoes

From the sixteenth century onwards, the art of war was at the heart of the production of numerous models that were aimed at furnishing sovereigns and soldiers with the most faithful representations possible of the fortified cities that defended each state along its borders.

The collection of *plans-reliefs* of Louis XIV of France (r. 1643–1715), which was initiated in 1668 and expanded and enriched until 1870, was the most prestigious in Europe on account of its size and the precision with which it was executed. The term *plan-relief* first appeared in the nineteenth century as a contraction of *plan en relief* (plan in relief), which, together with the words *modèle*, *relief* and even *plan*, had been used throughout the seventeenth and eighteenth centuries to describe the three-dimensional scale models of fortified cities created for Louis XIV.

Some 250 relief maps of fortified cities and forts were made between 1668 and 1870. Today, ninety-one are in the collection of the Musée des Plans-Reliefs at the Hôtel National des Invalides in Paris. These particular models are unique because they represent not only the precise layout of the fortifications, the details of all the buildings, the gardens and secondary elements such as fences and statues, but also the surrounding countryside, with its villages, farms and bridges. The vast territory around the fortified cities was reproduced in the scale models because it was within the range of artillery fire and offensive works constructed for siege warfare. As the range of artillery fire increased over the centuries, the territory represented on the models also grew.

Therefore, while *plans-reliefs* realized under Louis XIV measure approximately 20 square metres (215 sq. ft), those built during the later eighteenth century measure about 40 square metres (430 sq. ft) and those made around the middle of the nineteenth century have an average area of 70 square metres (753 sq. ft). In order to represent all of the architectural and landscape elements, the scale of 1 foot for 100 *toises*, or approximately 1:600, was used; that is to say, 1 centimetre on the model corresponds to 6 metres in reality. A more detailed scale was sometimes used to reproduce less extensive sites, such as isolated forts.

These landscape duplicates were originally military strategy tools belonging to the field of relief cartography. To provide an accurate and measurable representation of places, the scale used was the same for the city and the landscape, in plan and in

The plan-relief *of Besançon, France, constructed between 1720 und 1722, is built at 1:600 scale and is more than 6 metres (19½ ft) in length.*

elevation. It was important for military engineers to be aware of the characteristics of the landscape on which they were to lay out fortifications, and it was particularly crucial to know which heights dominated the sites to be defended and could therefore represent a danger.

At a time when it was impossible to have an aerial vision of a city or a landscape, and when flat mapping did not allow for the accurate depiction of the nature and importance of the landscape, these models were a great asset for topographical representation. They continued to be so in later times, because they permitted an immediate understanding of the organization of cities and their fortifications, of a land and the variations in its altitude, and thus they provided a global view of a site from multiple perspectives; they were truly a precursor of Google Earth.

The topography of the sites was reproduced on the basis of field surveys conducted first by military engineers and then, from the middle of the eighteenth century, by the topographical artists of the Galerie des Plans-Reliefs (as the organization was known from 1700, when the collection was transferred to the Louvre; in 1777 it was moved to Les Invalides, where the museum opened in 1943). All architectural and landscape elements were mapped, together with their altitude, and drawn on blueprints. Each blueprint was then used as the plan of a specific *plan-relief*.

At the same time, elevation drawings of all constructions (buildings in towns and villages, hamlets, isolated farms, castles) were recorded in notebooks, with notes regarding the nature and colours of the different elements (walls, roofs, streets, paths). The notebooks also indicated soil use (meadows, ploughed fields, salt marshes, vineyards, hop fields) and the presence of trees, bushes or groves. These drawings were made at the same scale as the *plans-reliefs*. In addition, watercolours were painted in order to record the colours of the landscape. These preparatory graphic documents are preserved only for the *plans-reliefs* produced during the nineteenth century. Sometimes samples of sand and rock were taken so as to render the landscape faithfully.

Because of their large size, the *plans-reliefs* consist of several wooden panels – called tables – fitted together like a giant puzzle. The upper part of a table consists of an assembly of strips of wood of different thicknesses, carved so as to reproduce the irregularities of the terrain, the details of which were modelled in papier mâché. Oil paint was used to represent water. The finish of the ground surface was obtained by spraying fine sand over a layer of glue. Dyed and finely powdered silk flock represents fields, meadows and open spaces. Trees were made of fine silk chenille interwoven with wire. The artists worked hard to represent the countryside, the various crops and different tree species with great realism; such details provided information to the military about resources available around a fortress.

It was indeed vital for the military to know not only details of the crops that could supply garrisons and armies in the field, but also about communication channels or barriers located around the fortified cities, such as woods, hedges, promontories and marshes.

Architectural elements of towns, villages and hamlets were carved in blocks of limewood, covered with printed or painted paper imitating the textures and colours of the various building materials, then arranged on the tables. Openings were cut out and features such as chimneys and windows added. Once the different tables of each *plan-relief* were ready, they were assembled. To conceal the joins between the tables, their outline followed details in the landscape, such as roads, waterways and field boundaries.

Plans-reliefs provide significant information about infrastructure in rural areas, and reflect changes in patterns of land use. They also allow the study of communication channels through the representation of roads, paths, rivers and canals, bridges and, in the nineteenth century, railways. Thanks to these detailed models, the museum's collection offers invaluable testimony to the characteristics of fortified cities and their peri-urban landscape between the late seventeenth and late nineteenth centuries.

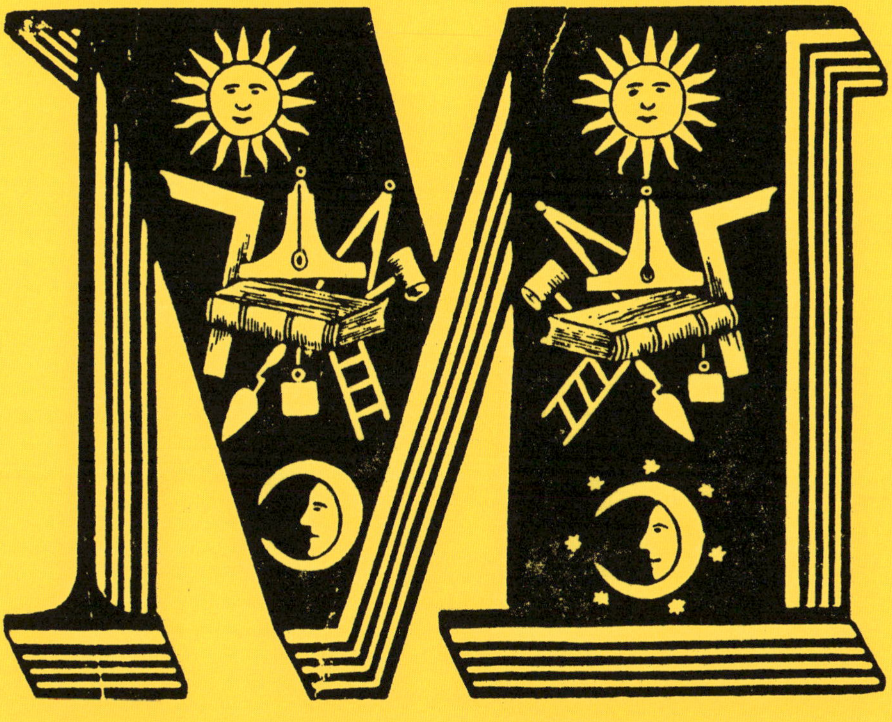

Making
George Rome Innes

Making: where does one start? Four thousand years ago, one would take a bolus of clay from the banks of the Nile and fashion a house the size of a coconut to take to one's grave as a habitation for the afterlife. If one was a person of means, one would employ a carpenter to make a model house in timber, using saws, planes and chisels. It might have been slightly grander than one's earthly home, but one needs to be comfortable in the afterlife. In both cases, the model house needed to be designed; some sort of specification or even drawings would have to be provided by whomever commissioned the model. The clay model might have been created from an idea in the maker's mind, but a timber model needed a drawing to convey the idea to the craftsman.

The architectural model falls into a number of categories: the sketch model, the structural model and the presentation model. The sketch model is made by the designer, who almost invariably first makes rough drawings on paper. To convert these sketches into a three-dimensional object, decisions need to be made about size. By necessity, sketch models have to be made quickly in simple materials, such as paper, card, foam board and balsa wood, using simple tools – scalpels and craft knives – and straight edges. Accuracy is not that important; this is about folding, cutting and gluing. It is the final effect that is key, as it helps the designer to realize a form in three dimensions.

Architectural models are made both to test the aesthetics of a building and to test the structure. Most of this testing is now done via digital modelling, but before the advent of computers, structural engineers used physical models to understand how structures would behave. Tests performed on the models included stress tests to establish acceptable levels of deformation, catenary tests to work out the most stable shapes of arches, and wind-tunnel tests to model the structural integrity of a building under extreme weather conditions or the effect a large building would have on the microclimate.

The presentation model once had to be made by a craftsman, but these days can also be made by a machine controlled by a program written by a designer or technician. The craftsman first requires a set of drawings that clearly represent the designer's idea. The scale and appearance must be decided. What is the model for? Is it to explain to a client the beauty or utility of the designer's vision? Is it to show a committee of councillors and residents how a new building will enhance their neighbourhood? Is it to pull the wool over their eyes? Early presentation models, made between the sixteenth and nineteenth centuries, were usually built by

Model at ¼-inch scale of Lord Burlington's Chiswick House (built 1726–29), made of limewood with cherry veneer by George Rome Innes and Network Modelmakers.

cabinetmakers and carpenters, and constructed in their workshops using timber and the tools of their trade.

In the nineteenth and the first half of the twentieth centuries, models were painted in what were deemed to be 'realistic' colours. But as a model is a miniature version of reality, it is a distant view. In the distance, colours are paler and softer – think of 'blue remembered hills'. Models look more realistic if the colours are cooler and paler than those that we see at close range.

These models were made using machine tools – circular saws, bandsaws and lathes – and some hand tools. The appearance of the materials was not important as long as the surface could take the paints, so timber was used initially, but when Perspex became available it provided the ideal smooth surface to which one could apply colour and texture.

By the 1980s, ideas had changed, and many models were monochromatic. This fashion was originally led by the reintroduction of plain timber models from various in-house model shops in London. To a certain extent, models were more abstract, and appealed to a client who was more versed in the language of design.

To produce the requisite fine finishes on unadorned timber models, new blades were developed for circular saws. Such saws were used not only to cut simple shapes, but also to make delicate mouldings. The most popular woods were lime (or basswood), yellow cedar and tulip tree, all of which have a fine, almost imperceptible grain. Sometimes the monochromatic palette was broken by the use of American black walnut, red cedar, cherry and harewood.

Fashions changed again, and as the 'high-tech' architecture of Norman Foster and Richard Rogers came to the fore, white models followed. To start with, many of the same techniques were employed as earlier, but acrylic and polystyrene became the materials of choice. More fluid forms arose, resulting in the use of vacuum forming as a production method. Metal etching, initially used in the jewellery industry, was also applied to model-making, and items of unbelievable delicacy could be produced.

With technological advances in computer science, laser-cutting and 3D printing have become commonplace in the trade of architectural model-making. The very best example using almost all these methods in a single project has been the restoration of the fearsome dragons on the Great Pagoda at Kew Gardens in south-west London. The pagoda was designed by Sir William Chambers and completed in 1762. Each of the ten storeys had a family of eight dragons made of solid pine, with the highest storey having the smallest dragons, and the lowest those on the grandest scale. By 1784, however, all the original dragons had flown; they were taken down, either because they were too heavy for the structure or because the wood had rotted. As the first step of the restoration project that began in 2014, sketches were made of chinoiserie dragons of the mid-eighteenth century; these were followed by a clay model, and then a master pattern was carved in timber in the traditional way. The wooden model was scanned, and the first copy printed in three dimensions. With the click of a few buttons, the scale could be changed, and so nine families of dragons of increasing dimensions were formed in a vat of liquid resin as the laser beam solidified the plastic.

The dragons on the ground storey were a special case, carved from cedar using hand tools with a history that dates back millennia. But even here modern techniques were used. To make such a complicated form in timber, the object was roughed out in a series of blocks, which were cut using a computer-aided method and then glued firmly together. Once glued, the blocks were trimmed with a chainsaw before the expert craftsman Paul Jewby picked up razor-sharp chisels to produce a work of art.

Architectural models have been made of almost every material: clay for a home for eternity; ivory, ebony and olive wood for devotional models of the Church of the Holy Sepulchre; oak, lime and beech for the original models of the great Renaissance cathedrals (which are often the only evidence of what might have been, had the architect's intentions been realized); timber and paint in the nineteenth and twentieth centuries; and plastics and etched metals today. Model-making tools have ranged from basic ancient hand tools, which are still in use, to machine tools and the wonders of computer-aided manipulation. But, in the end, it is the skill of the maker that produces the model.

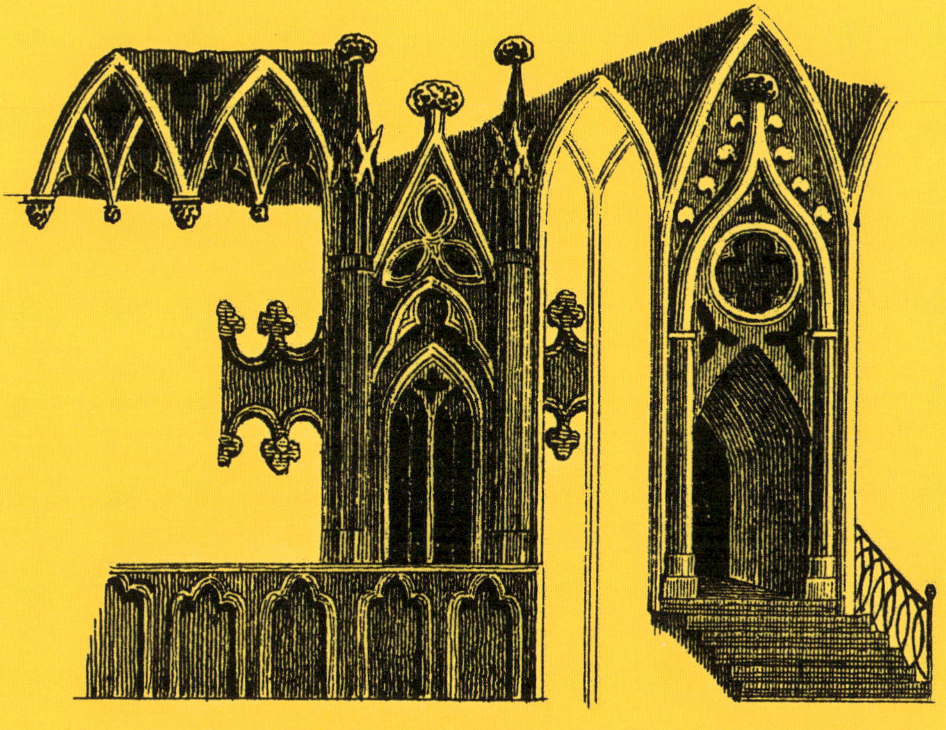

Narrative
Nikos Magouliotis

During the nineteenth century, Jerusalem was part of the Ottoman Empire. Like many other cities within the empire's vast territory stretching from the Middle East to the Balkans, it was home to different Muslim, Jewish and Christian ethnicities who lived together and practised their religions in close proximity. The buildings in which such practices took place – the numerous ancient and modern religious monuments of Jerusalem – were frequently highly contested sites that required the constant negotiation of religious, territorial and often architectural borders between the local religious communities and authorities.

The monumental complex of the Church of the Holy Sepulchre, in the Christian Quarter of the Old City of Jerusalem, was perhaps the seminal example of such a site. Its core, built in the fourth century CE, had grown over the centuries and through numerous additions into a complex architectural agglomeration; a religious ecosystem whose different parts were owned and occupied by different Christian denominations and ethnicities, as well as by the Muslim authorities. As with many other religious sites in Jerusalem and Bethlehem, the property division of the Holy Sepulchre – which particular ethnicity and denomination owned each of its numerous chapels and sanctuaries, as well as who could use each space for their ceremonies, and at what time – was regulated by what is known as the 'Status Quo', an old oral agreement between the different religious communities of the city. From 1757,

Engraving from the Illustrirte Zeitung *of one of Conrad Schick's models of the Holy Sepulchre on display in Stuttgart in 1863.*

the agreement was reinforced in written form through a firman (decree) issued by the Ottoman sultan Osman III. Through many more firmans and diplomatic efforts, the local authorities and the central government of the Ottoman Empire in Istanbul continued their attempts to quell the conflicts around the Holy Sepulchre by dictating the preservation of the architectural complex in its current state. But arguments would still arise when it came to the maintenance and repair of its different parts.

A culmination of these conflicts in the early 1860s led the Ottoman governor of Jerusalem, Süreyya Pasha, to arrive at a rather architectural solution. He decided that the best way to visualize and forever solidify the property division of the Holy Sepulchre would be to construct a three-dimensional scale model of the complex. This delicate technical and diplomatic task was bestowed on Conrad Schick (1822–1901), a German craftsman and missionary who had arrived in Jerusalem in the 1840s as part of the Swiss mission of St Chrischona in Basel. Schick had little experience in architecture or models, but his extensive training in different crafts and his status as a relative outsider to the conflict – German Protestants had no claims on the Holy Sepulchre – made him a perfect candidate for the task. After extensive surveys and measurements of the building complex, in 1862 Schick condensed all his knowledge of the Holy Sepulchre's architecture and ownership division into a wooden model at a scale of 1:96 and measuring 132 × 175 centimetres (52 × 69 in.).* The most striking feature of the model, its diagrammatic polychromy, is a direct result of the purpose for which it was made. Its different colours represent the Christian denominations that owned the different parts of the complex: blue for Greek Orthodox, brown for Roman Catholics, yellow for Armenians, green for Copts and white for the parts that were common property. But the model has another, equally interesting feature: it is constructed as a three-dimensional jigsaw puzzle of moveable parts. The roofs, walls and other building parts can be removed and taken apart in order to allow for views into the interior of the labyrinthine complex, and for close examination of the property divisions of its spaces, even in the case of small chapels and alcoves.

Schick's model of the Holy Sepulchre in Jerusalem (1862) on display in the exhibition In Statu Quo: Structures of Negotiation *at the Tel Aviv Museum of Art, 2019.*

This object of almost mechanical perfection and precision – made by Schick, who, among other things, was trained in manufacturing clock mechanisms – was intended as the ultimate guarantee of the agreement between the different Christian ethnicities and denominations and the local Muslim authorities. It was the final stage of consolidation of the Status Quo: from an oral contract to a written decree and then to a miniature architectural form. Through Schick's model, the monumental Holy Sepulchre became small enough to be placed on a table; a negotiation table, around which governors, clergymen, diplomats and other officials could meet to argue, compromise or provoke. The easily moveable parts of the almost toylike Holy Sepulchre model allowed them to 'play' with this complex problem.

This allusion to playing, pedagogics and, by extension, toys might appear inappropriate in light of the often violent conflicts that the model sought to reconcile. But it is, in fact, related to the cultural background of its maker: Schick trained as a craftsman in southern Germany and Switzerland in the middle of the nineteenth century, a time when central Europe was witnessing a boom in various pedagogical miniatures, models and building kits. At the beginning of the century, German pedagogues had published model-making books for children and argued that the construction and study of miniature houses were essential aspects of geometrical and, more broadly, cultural education. In the following decades, school classrooms and households were equipped with such pedagogical architectural miniatures and kits, from the abstract geometric *Fröbelgaben* (Fröbel's Gifts) of Friedrich Fröbel (from the 1830s onwards) to the more figurative and architectural *Anker-Steinbaukästen* (Anchor Stone Building Sets; in the 1880s). Children were educated through models of biblical sites (from Nativity scenes to miniatures of Noah's Ark, equipped with figures of its human and animal passengers), and were encouraged to play with a variety of didactic and normative building kits or doll's houses.

Something of this toylike innocence – or, rather, the pedagogical and didactic simplification of an otherwise complex reality – seems to have seeped into the brightly coloured building kit of the Holy Sepulchre made by Schick in Jerusalem in 1862. If we were not aware of the tense religious and territorial debates that generated it, we could easily be led to believe that it was made for educational purposes. About a century after this model-making took place, Roland Barthes wrote in his essay collection *Mythologies* (1957) that toys are 'a microcosm of the adult world': they are made to prepare the child for it, and in doing so, they can 'reveal the list of all the things the adult does not find unusual: war, bureaucracy, ugliness, Martians, etc.' The 1862 model of the Holy Sepulchre seems to perform a similar function: by miniaturizing and diagramming this heavily conflicted site, it rendered innocuous the absurdity and violence that its division entailed, but also it allowed for architectural gestures that could have violent effects on the real-scale environment and life of Jerusalem.

*In 2019 the model was displayed in the exhibition *In Statu Quo: Structures of Negotiation* at the Tel Aviv Museum of Art, curated by Deborah Pinto Fdeda, Ifat Finkelman, Oren Sagiv and Tania Coen-Uzzielli. (The exhibition was originally shown in the Israeli Pavilion at the Venice Architecture Biennale of 2018.) The permanent position of the model appears to be in the Christ Church Heritage Centre in Jerusalem.

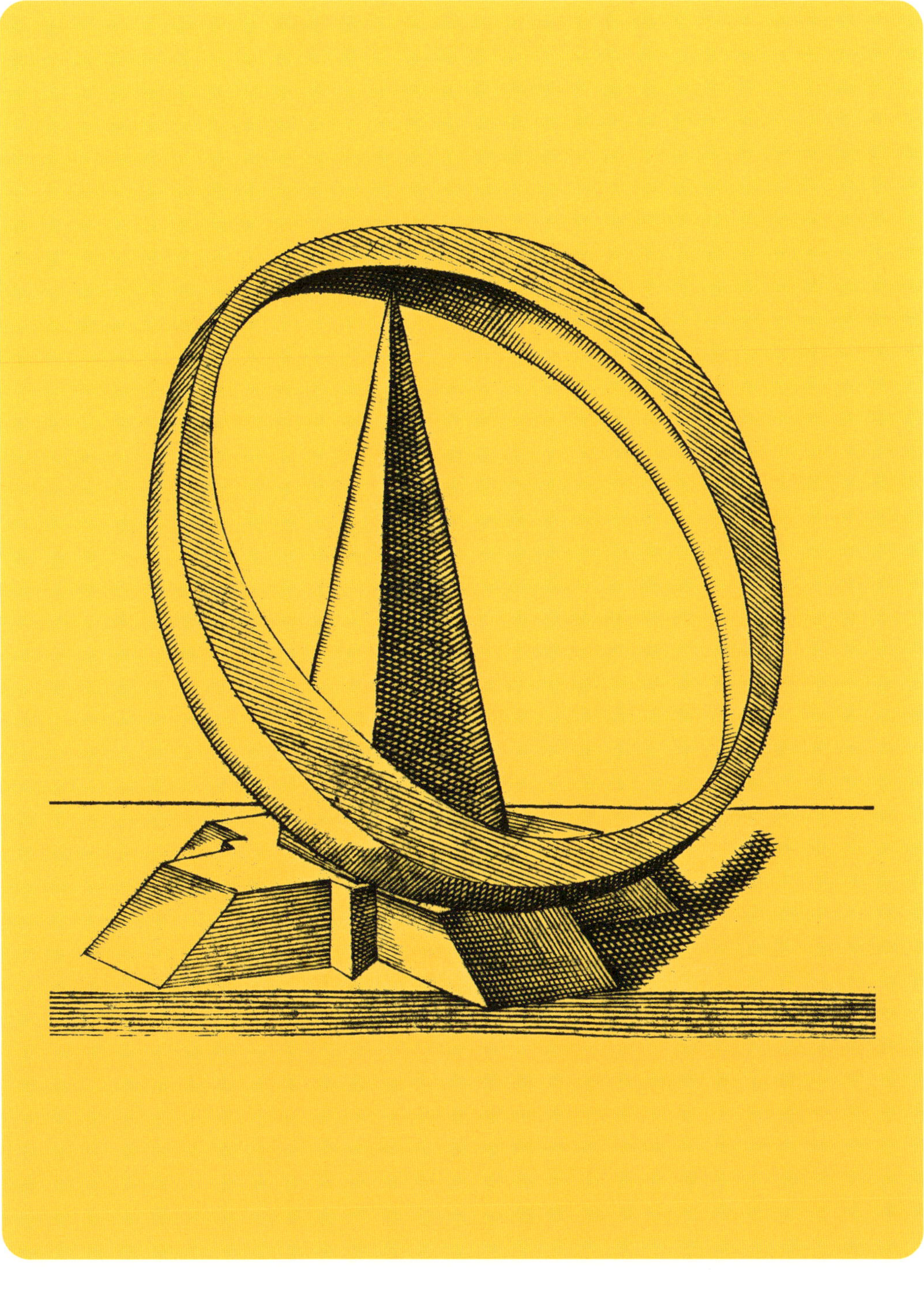

One to One
Mary S. Morgan

Alice's Adventures in Wonderland and *Through the Looking-Glass* hold many surprises, particularly Alice's experiences of scale – shrinking down to the size of a mushroom, or trying to squish her new giant-like frame through a doorway. Architects and scientists experience similar adventures in scale when they play around with sizes, dimensions and materials in their use of models. The variety of scales used in scientific modelling offers many parallels with questions of scale in architectural models.

Scale and Size
The reference point for all scale, of course, is one to one – that is, a direct correspondence between the size of the object and the size of the representation of it (often denoted as 1:1). But one to one is relatively limited in terms of its applications; it is, in fact, the ability to shift the ratio from one to one to a different value that makes models so flexible and versatile. Scientists and architects create models to bring the site of their research into perspective with their own human senses. For scientists, unlike architects, this means that some things are habitually modelled at a much bigger scale (for example, the molecular ball-and-spoke models of chemistry), and some are modelled at a much smaller scale than the objects those models represent (for example, the planetary system models created by early astronomers). An equally serious consideration is that the choice of scale is dependent on what the scientist or architect wants to learn from their model – that is, the particular purpose of the modelling. Both ask, is this model at the right scale for the job? Models are like maps in this respect: a walking map will differ in scale from both a driving map and an ocean-current map. But in all cases, the usability of the map depends on accurate information at that scale; map keys are critical. Just as maps that lack consistent use of a length or distance scale make them difficult to use for walking purposes, architectural models, too, may suffer from lack of information about scale, hiding the fact, for example, that some steps in a computer-aided model staircase would be metres high if actually built.

   Architects habitually model things at a smaller scale than the object they are designing, yet may use many different-scaled models of the same things in order to understand the different properties of their planned buildings and to suggest different experiences in the use of those buildings. Whereas (perhaps counter-intuitively to the scientist) smaller-scale models may be used to provide insights into large spatial arrangements, larger-scale models may prove more valuable for understanding the possibilities of details, and are also more malleable when it comes to assessing alterations. Both small- and large-scale models can lead to surprising results by revealing what does not work well in those very different design contexts.

Scale and Dimensionality

Models are like maps in another respect: they typically show only a limited number of things, not all the details of the territory. For scientists, this poses another type of scale problem: deciding how many dimensions of their phenomena should be represented in the model. Models of large open systems (such as the climate system), or ones with multiple sources of reaction (as in the modelling of infectious diseases in a pandemic), will present very different challenges. But they share the question: which of many elements and relations of the problem should be shown in a model? A model with too many dimensions – that is, too many variables and relations – may not be usable because of cognitive overload. At one stage, for example, statistical models of the whole economy became several hundred equations in size – difficult for one scientist to grasp, and equally difficult for teams of economists who each understood specific bits but had to integrate their knowledge with that of other team members.

Economist Walter Newlyn and engineer Bill Phillips built this hydraulic machine in 1949 to demonstrate the workings of the economy; here, Phillips stands by the prototype (Mark I) design.

Probably the most significant difference between architects and scientists lies in the latter's desire to accommodate what is called a 'timescale' in their models. Understanding what happens over time is an important problem for scientists, whether they work in the natural, social or human sciences, and they incorporate time in different ways in their choice of different modelling materials. For example, when biologists looked for a 'model organism' in their investigation of inheritance, they chose fruit flies (the pesky little black flies that hang about our fruit bowls) because those flies reproduce so rapidly that biologists can track genetic change easily, rather than having to wait for human population changes. The famous Newlyn–Phillips Hydraulic Machine model of the economy, devised in 1949, calibrated its circulation time of red liquid (money) around the tubes and tanks of the model in minutes, even though the real time of adjustments in the national economy that it sought to mimic could be weeks, months or years. In contrast, computer visualizations of models of chemical bonding slow down the process to explore, in slow motion, the plausible details of what are usually very fast chemical reactions. So, different timescales are chosen in relation both to the purposes of enquiry and to the dimensions relevant to the activity studied, be it the reproduction cycles of animals or the business cycles of society. It is perhaps less obvious what the equivalent use of time dimensions could be for architects. Maintenance cycles are often taken into account in modelling, but users of airports might well wonder if architects ever include in their models any consideration of the time it takes to walk from one end of a terminal building to the other.

Scale and Materials
Another important scale problem for scientists emerges in the choice of materials that make up the model in relation to the real-world materials that are being mimicked. Historians recount that when simulations of earthquakes were first undertaken in small-scale physical models, scientists had to figure out which materials would behave in a similar way to rock at that small scale: the answer was pancake batter. In a parallel case of a water-tank model used to assess the performance of transatlantic cables, the 'sea' had to be made considerably more viscose and treacle-like. These translations of materials to the smaller scale seem quite surprising: namely, that rocks would be translated into something liquid and seawater needed to be made thicker. There are surely equivalent issues in material scaling in architectural modelling. These might be questions about whether a cardboard model will behave as expected in real building materials, or whether computer-simulation assumptions will play out in real life. Will the concrete actually flow around that sharp corner as assumed in the model, or will the real cladding actually hook around that bend as seamlessly as paper does in the model? The behaviour of materials in the real world is not scale-independent, and architects as much as scientists must necessarily take this into account.

  For architects, the material qualities of models are bound up intrinsically with their aesthetic qualities. Architects will want to mimic the final appearance in their models in the respects they hold to be important. They will be concerned about how textures that look right in small-scale models in card will look good at full size in stone. Their aesthetic concerns about the model might be much broader, in fact, to include the relation to other buildings and the surrounding environment, and to take account of light or shade. To the scientist, architectural models that use polished wood to represent an intended stone plaza may strike a discordant note in terms of materials and visuality, while the use of matchsticks or balsa wood may suggest flimsiness. Of course, similar dissonance about materials may be experienced by architects when they find scientists representing, say, people's behaviour, or forest growth, in mathematical equations. For both architects and scientists, model-building is a project of interaction with an artefact, but perhaps for scientists, that interaction is not primarily an experiential-aesthetic one – as it must be with the humanistic artefacts of architectural models.

A square of paper is folded ▢ and cut → ☐ ☐ and opened like this

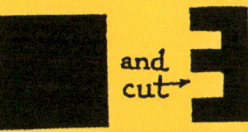

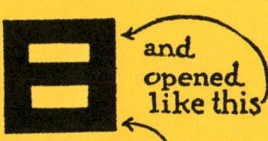

The alphabet has been made from this form

P

This cut-out alphabet is easily made and makes an attractive arrangement when used on poster work. All of the letters are cut from the window shape at the top of the page.

Paper
Giovanni Santucci

Paper has been used for centuries in architectural model-making. The reasons are clear: since the fifteenth century it has been a material always in the possession of artists and architects for their drawing activity; it was, and remains, relatively inexpensive; its use requires no special equipment; and it can easily be manipulated into many regular and irregular solid forms widely employed in architecture, such as cubes, pyramids, cylinders and even segmented hemispheres. In the early modern period, purposefully sized and shaped drawings on paper were sometimes pasted on to architectural models otherwise made of wood as an expedient way of adding ornamental details that would have required much time and money to be carved in relief. Some of the most ambitious wooden models produced in Italy between the sixteenth and eighteenth centuries are finished in such a way. For instance, the inner walls of a model for the cross of Como Cathedral made by Cristoforo Solari in 1519 (Museo Civico, Como) are papered with shaded drawings reproducing carvings and inlays of marble, while the barrel vaults of the wooden model by Antonio da Sangallo the Younger for the new St Peter's Basilica (1539–46; Museo della Fabbrica di San Pietro, Vatican City) are lined with drawings imitating an *all'antica* pattern of variously shaped coffers. Drawings on paper, in this case coloured, also complete one of the models by Bernardo Buontalenti for the façade of Florence Cathedral (1580s; Museo dell'Opera del Duomo, Florence) and one half of a huge model by Filippo Juvarra for the sacristy of St Peter's (1714; Museo della Fabbrica di San Pietro).

The early modern period was also the first Golden Age of three-dimensional architectural models made only, or mainly, of paper. The use of paper models is documented in Tuscany since at least the beginning of the sixteenth century, and soon spread to the main artistic centres of northern and central Italy and also, although only occasionally, abroad. These design tools, usually called *modelli di cartone* in Italian textual sources, were assembled by cutting out and gluing a particular type of orthographic drawing in which all the main surfaces of an architectural structure were developed in plane and then edge-joined one to another. The bulk of the paper models that have come down to us, normally preserved unfolded and therefore stored as if they were ordinary architectural drawings, are relatively small and have a simple box-like appearance, with most of the smaller secondary volumes reproduced in an illusionary way with the help of shading and colour. This is the case with a paper model by Federico Brandani for the barrel-vaulted Chapel of the Dukes of Urbino in the Sanctuary of Loreto (1564; Ashmolean Museum, Oxford), as well as with many others for façades or the decoration of rooms. A few paper models are a little more complex, such as one by Baldassarre Peruzzi for the interior restoration of the church of San Domenico in Siena (1536; Galleria degli Uffizi, Florence) and others reproducing segmented domes and coved vaults. Documentary evidence, however, makes it clear that some now-lost paper models were of a considerable size and assembled from many different parts supported by hidden stays. One such example is a paper model for which Galeazzo Alessi was paid in 1569; it showed both the outside and inside of his project for the church of Santa Maria Assunta di Carignano in Genoa. Other examples include the paper models made by Guarino Guarini, Gian Lorenzo Bernini and Filippo Juvarra to promote their projects for, respectively, the dome of the church of San Vincenzo in Modena (1653), the Spanish Steps in Rome (1660s) and a gallery in the Royal Palace in Madrid (1736).

Whether large or small, complex or simple, in the period under consideration, paper models fulfilled the same purposes as other kinds of architectural models, especially that of allowing architects to communicate with those patrons who were not able to understand the spatial features of a project only by looking at drawings. Although they were less effective than models made of wood, clay or wax in communicating the three-dimensionality of a designed building at a small scale, paper models could nevertheless represent in a clearer and

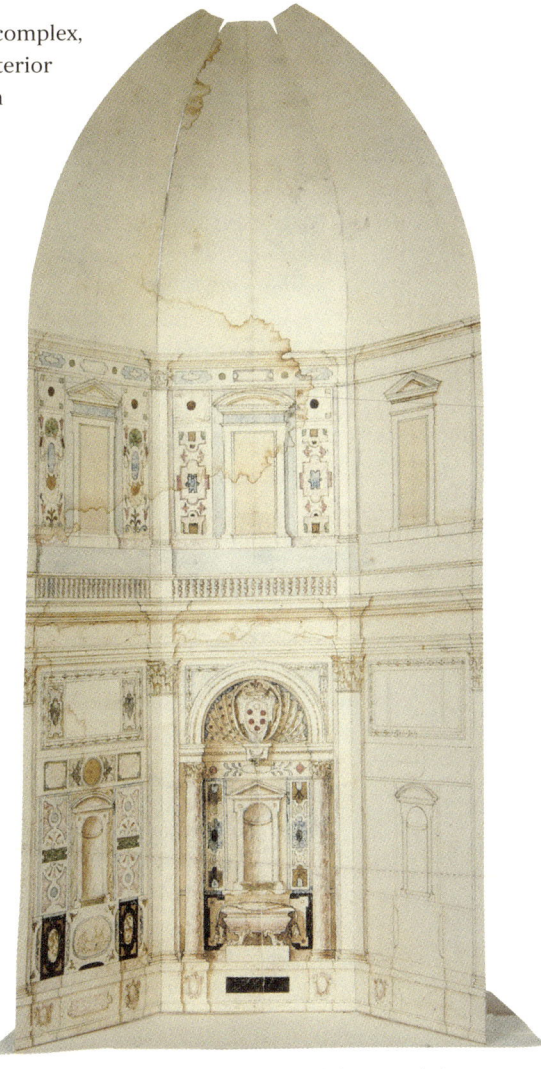

Paper model by Alessandro Pieroni showing a design for the interior decoration of the Cappella dei Principi in the basilica of San Lorenzo, Florence (1602–1604).

more easily measurable way even the minor features of the architectural surface and of the decoration. Their manufacture was economic and efficient, two qualities that encouraged their use in architectural design competitions. In addition, the use of paper allowed any architect to produce several models for the same building, and thus they could be compared side by side and discussed with the patron, a practice that emerged particularly at the Medici court in the late sixteenth century. In the Tuscan artistic environment, which, under the influence of Michelangelo's thought, conceived of art and beauty as a matter of direct perception, paper models could assist the creative process. A group of paper models manufactured from rough sketches by Alessandro Pieroni, Giovanni Antonio Dosio and Bernardo Buontalenti (Galleria degli Uffizi; Biblioteca Nazionale Centrale, Florence) show how these tools were used to form visual judgements, rather than the architects making rule-based design decisions, in experimental solutions for the Cappella Niccolini (in the basilica of Santa Croce; 1584), the Cappella dei Principi (in the basilica of San Lorenzo; 1602–1604) and other similarly significant buildings in Florence.

Paper models were also useful when information about an architectural project had to be sent abroad. In such cases, a three-dimensional demonstration of the design was usually required to compensate for the absence of the architect. Wooden or clay models were heavy and impractical for shipping, whereas light models made of paper were ideal for that purpose, and in some cases may even have been sent simply as flat sheets.

Finally, from the sixteenth to the eighteenth century, architectural models in paper were also made by major Italian painters – Giorgio Vasari, Federico Zuccari (Galleria degli Uffizi; The Metropolitan Museum of Art, New York), Giovanni Guerra (Biblioteca Comunale, Palermo; National Gallery of Art, Washington, D.C.) and Giovanni Francesco Romanelli (Ashmolean Museum), among others – as a means by which to reflect on the overall effect of ambitious groups of wall paintings and for presentation to patrons.

By the second half of the eighteenth century, paper models had apparently begun to seem an inadequate tool to represent buildings adorned, according to the emerging classical taste, with columns and other purely volumetric ornaments. Over the course of the nineteenth century, paper was thus mainly relegated to the production of educational or toy architectural models for children, while for their professional needs architects made almost exclusive use of sophisticated sets of coloured and shaded elevations and sections on paper and, especially in competitions for public buildings, of wood or cast-plaster models. In the second half of the century, the custom of papering the inside of presentation wooden models with drawings was sometimes revived, particularly in Britain: to give just one example, in a model by Captain Francis Fowke for the Royal Albert Hall (1864; Victoria and Albert Museum, London; see p. 4). A handbook of 1859 by T.A. Richardson, *The Art of Architectural Modelling in Paper*, also taught architects how to produce models using only multilayered pasteboard, but in fact, because this material was very thick and had to be worked with tools in order to render even the smallest details in relief, it did not, in any real sense, differ from wood. Therefore, it was only in the first decades of the twentieth century – when many architects in different countries began to think of architecture in terms of solid masses of pure geometric volumes, and to regard models as a central element of the design process rather than a representation of the final design – that simple folded paper was again seen as an extremely suitable material for model-making. The construction of paper models assisted the volumetric explorations of some of the greatest masters of modern architecture, such as Le Corbusier, Mies van der Rohe and Frank Gehry, and it still remains a well-established part of the regular training of architecture students worldwide.

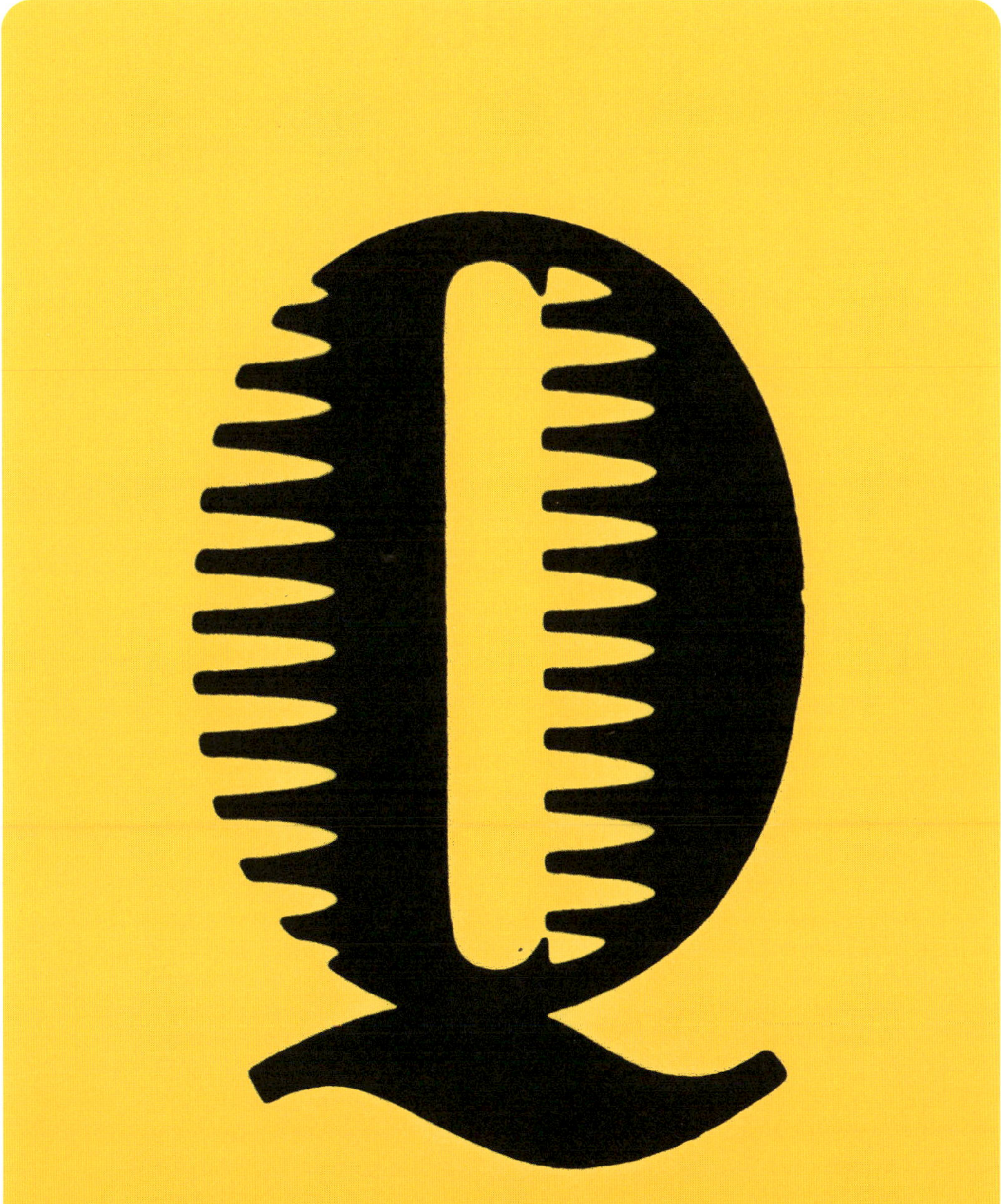
Q

Quick
Rawden Pettitt

Quick: 'moving fast or doing something in a short time'. This definition is a state of affairs that we architects constantly seek to avoid in our working lives. We crave the space and time to evaluate carefully and to develop our thoughts with creativity and rigour. However, as technology and expectations continue to evolve, we become more pressured by time constraints across all facets of our work.

Three-dimensional CAD models, renderings and fly-throughs are now commonplace in the architect's office, and often replace physical drawings and models. Physical model-making is increasingly supplemented by laser cutters and 3D printers, and computer-generated imagery of ever-increasing 'realism' extends the visual image's dominance of architectural culture at the expense of other modes of perception. These tools have greatly increased the capacity for production, the sophistication of presentations, and the ability to define complex geometries, but they have a fundamental impact on both the way we design and the resulting architecture. As Juhani Pallasmaa says in *The Eyes of the Skin* (1996), his study of the relationship between architecture and the senses, 'The computer creates a distance between the maker and the object, whereas drawing by hand as well as model-making put the designer into a haptic contact with the object or space.'

Architectural technology is one facet of a world that is increasingly virtual and mediated through the digital. While these technologies have become essential to the way we live and design, in this context the physical and real become more, not less, valuable. As architects, we are engaged in the encounter between people and the physical world; how people experience place, and how place affects them. Model-making is the first step towards understanding this reality. Working with card, plaster, stone, wood, steel and glass is a bridge to understanding the material presence of a building. Exploring the subtle unfolding of spaces and play of light is a way of 'being there' and sensing the feel of the spaces we are designing in all their tactile and sensory complexity.

From this, one could perhaps infer that model-making is about the reintroduction of slowness into the design process. However, we as a studio do not believe that to be entirely true. There is also great value in the act of making with speed: witness the study model or maquette – the quick model. We take a pencil and make marks on paper. We take pieces of card and hold them together, reconfigure, cut, pin, add, fold, subtract, assemble, carve, disassemble, reassemble. In each case, the hand thinks. Sometimes there is a mistake. One sketch collides with another to create something unexpected. A broken model suggests a new spatial arrangement.

Accidents are an essential part of our process. This is the reason why we make quick models. Making by hand explores thoughts that are unpremeditated, preverbal, non-linear. The idea evolves before the brain has had time to set boundaries or enforce preconceptions.

In our studio, this is an integral part of the design process. By being able to manipulate an object physically with our hands, we are not making it easier to think; we are thinking, whether the actions are deliberate or serendipitous. This phenomenon forms the basis of the theory of embodied cognition, which supposes that the act of thinking is an activity embedded in a physical environment, as opposed to existing within an abstract or disembodied mind. We rely on the senses of our entire body and not just the mind for such cognitive tasks as reasoning and making a judgement. By engaging in the act of model-making, as opposed to the more removed activity of simply viewing a completed, refined or even virtual model, we believe we can more immediately understand the implications of actions and more efficiently reach design resolutions. It is the craft of making things, be they drawings or models, that is the essence of design.

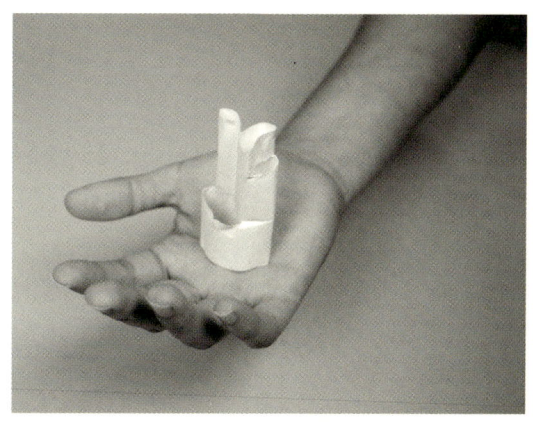

Sketch figurine in paper by Stanton Williams for the Riverwalk apartment complex, London, 2016.

Although we produce a wide range of model types in our studio, to satisfy various needs, each of our projects begins as a collection of primitive modelling materials strewn across a table. Once our understanding of the programme and site has evolved, we explore opportunities and test ideas with such rudimentary items as blades, glue, pins and tape. Technology in the form of laser cutters and 3D printers of course offers a further range of possibilities for the 'quick' model; however, for us its value relates purely to the attainment of speed, compared to what the process can offer when done by hand.

These physical studies allow us to share our spatial explorations

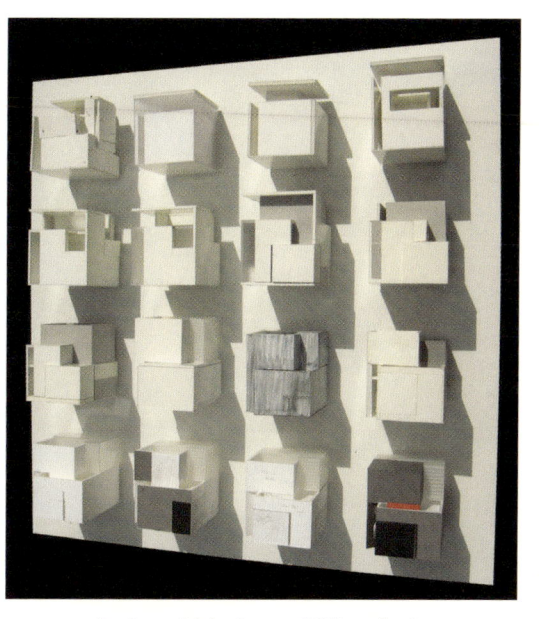

Study models by Stanton Williams for the Belgrade Theatre, Coventry, 2007.

with others: team members, clients, users and consultants. Design is collaborative. Discussion while gathered around design models allows everyone to engage with the design of spaces and to contribute to the creative process. These models help us to make design issues visible in the most tangible manner for all those involved – a significant advantage when CAD drawing means that designers spend so much time at their own computers. They allow us to respond in real time to the wider effects of manipulation or variation, and offer opportunities for a wide variety of perspectives. Such models provide a shared focus for design discussion in a way that promotes interaction, the exchange of ideas, and engagement with the messy, physical, creative process of designing the world in which we live.

The quick study model can also evolve. It is not precious. It is a tool. It may be dismembered, added to or duplicated as an exploration of options. It can also be incorporated into alternative media that follow the same principle of utilizing quick acts of manipulation in order to solve problems and help develop proposals. Simple photographs of card arrangements become backdrops for us to layer numerous freehand sketches over, exploring the potential for greater levels of detail. Or often these photographs become the foundation layer in a Photoshop program to help us quickly produce a concept of an evolved form, which is especially beneficial during design competitions.

Long after our projects have reached completion, our archive of study models, those that help to define the journey taken, remain as references we celebrate.

This essay is based on the article 'Why Make Models?', by Gavin Henderson, Principal Director at Stanton Williams, published in *The Architects' Journal*, 22 January 2016.

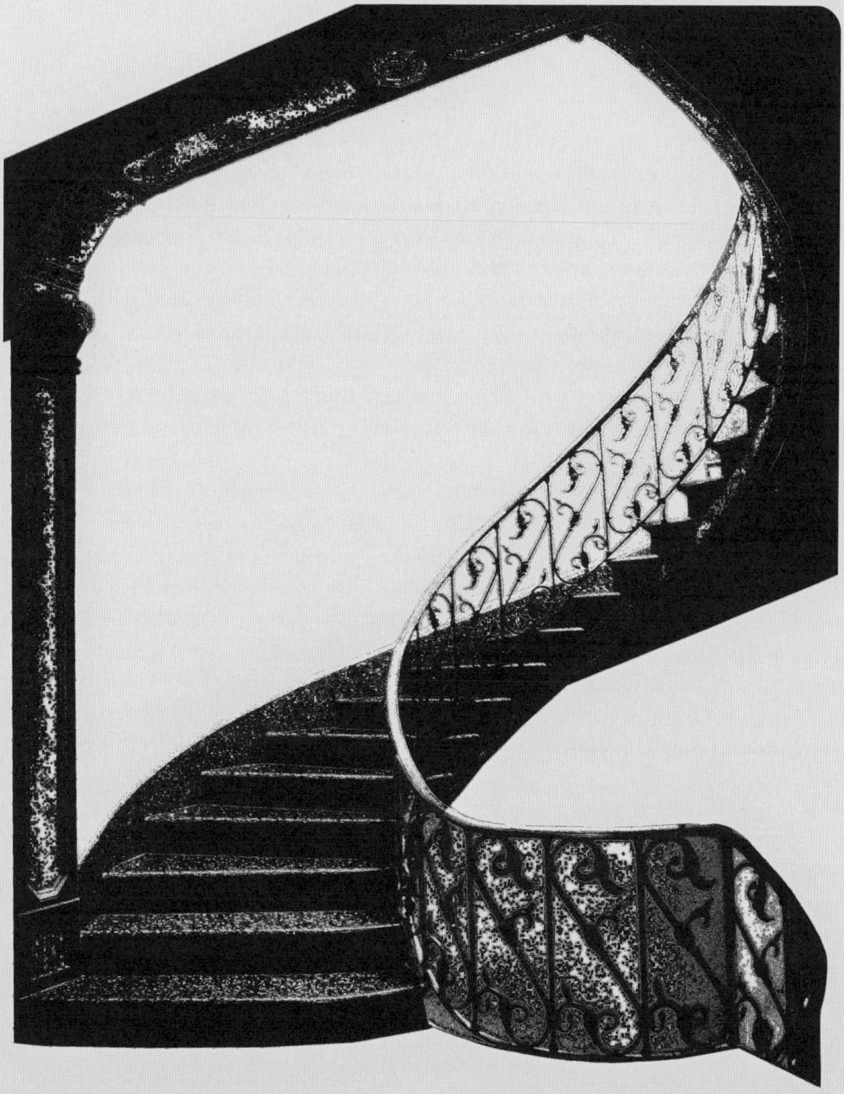

Representation
Ralf Liptau

When it comes to analysing the status and function of architectural and design models, the concept of representation is central because it underlines the core idea of what these artefacts are: they stand for something else. They are a symbol, a first materialization, a placeholder for abstract ideas, for constructions and forms. They are thus communicative or epistemic tools. All models represent a material or immaterial 'something'. It is the principal reason for their existence. This understanding of models allows us to categorize, to analyse and to describe what exactly each different kind of model does, can do or ought to do. To think about what representation through models is, means to think about what models are. Two fundamental questions stand out: *what* shall be represented by the model? And, *why* by the model?

So, what is it that is to be represented by the material artefact called the model? It depends. Within the fields of architecture and design, we can set apart two main types of model: those that are involved with design processes and actively shape them, and those that serve as replicas of already completed architectural and design concepts, be they realized or not. A distinctive example of models used as tools within the architectural design process are those made by Eero Saarinen during the design of the TWA Flight Center at Idlewild Airport (now JFK Airport) in New York. The terminal is well known for its spectacular non-Euclidean shape, which could be said to symbolize wings and the weightlessness of air travel. In 1958, four years before its opening, the building was praised in the journal *L'Architecture d'aujourd'hui* for its 'deliberate rupture' with 'every kind of orthogonal rationalism'. In 1960 Helmut Borcherdt, a former member of Saarinen's staff, explained in the journal *Baukunst und Werkform*, 'It would be impossible to carry out such a design without a model. The representation of buildings on paper is only a tool of communication; it tells nothing about the spatial qualities of a building. The design language will probably be influenced by the medium with which one has worked during the design.' Borcherdt here connects representational aspects of the model with its productive potential as a non-human 'actor' that – in interaction with the design team – develops in a certain direction to create a design that had not previously existed.

Concepts of 'tacit knowledge', of the productive mixing of 'making and thinking', even the idea of science and play, raise another question concerning the concept of representation: what exactly is it that a model represents, when it does not stand for something already extant? Moreover, what happens when it interacts with others during the design process and thus influences its own development and shape? Models that are integrated in a design process obviously gain specific importance both during this process and for the process. The artefacts that are left at the end of the process represent these ways of thinking as a reminder, a remainder, or sometimes only as trash. They are not created in order to represent an object developed or even realized elsewhere. The artefact is a leftover of the process, not really representing but rather bearing witness to what has happened.

Expectations concerning models and representation are easier to tackle when it comes to models produced in order to make visible, to communicate or to promote a thing or design that already exists. Examples include presentation models for architectural concepts or newly developed car bodies, both of which share some characteristics with didactical models in a scientific context. They all make visible something that either has existed, exists (but is too small, too big or too far away to be observed) or shall exist. They claim to be reliable replicas of something else and thus to be able to represent the main characteristics of this 'something else', be they visual characteristics or other analogies.

This leads to the question, why is something represented by a model, either during the design process or to make visible a thing that is already extant? And

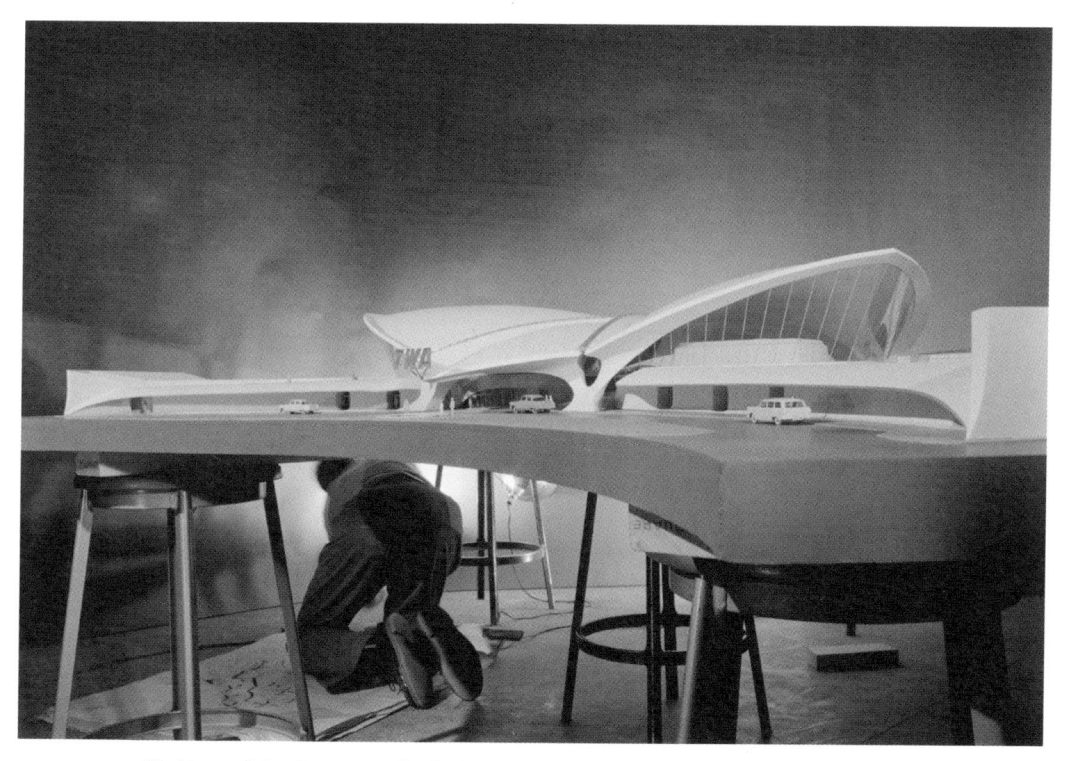

Working model under construction for Eero Saarinen's Trans World Airlines (TWA) Flight Center at Idlewild Airport, New York (1958–62), photographed by Balthazar Korab.

what is the core potential of models when it comes to questions of representation – for example, in comparison to sketches and drawings? The main characteristic is obvious: a model presents its 'content' in three dimensions. It is an artefact that can be taken in one's hands, turned around and looked at from several perspectives. In many cases, it can be manipulated or disassembled. It is an artefact in the 'real' world, not just in the constructed environment of a two-dimensional picture, and thus it promises a strong resemblance to what it represents. On the other hand, it always has to maintain a certain otherness in order not to be redundant; the difference concerns either time or space. The model must either be smaller, bigger or lighter than what it represents. Or it has to be prior, subsequent or more permanent. Whatever the type of model, this field of tension between otherness and similarity is something they all have to deal with. The productivity that lies in the – sometimes closer, sometimes wider – link between model and 'original' contributes to the core potential of models and their different modes of representation.

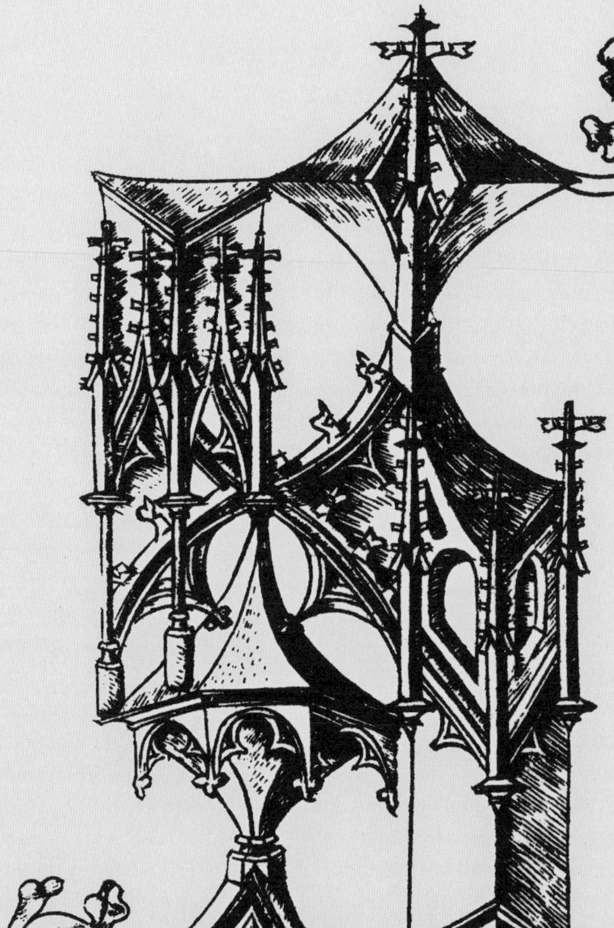

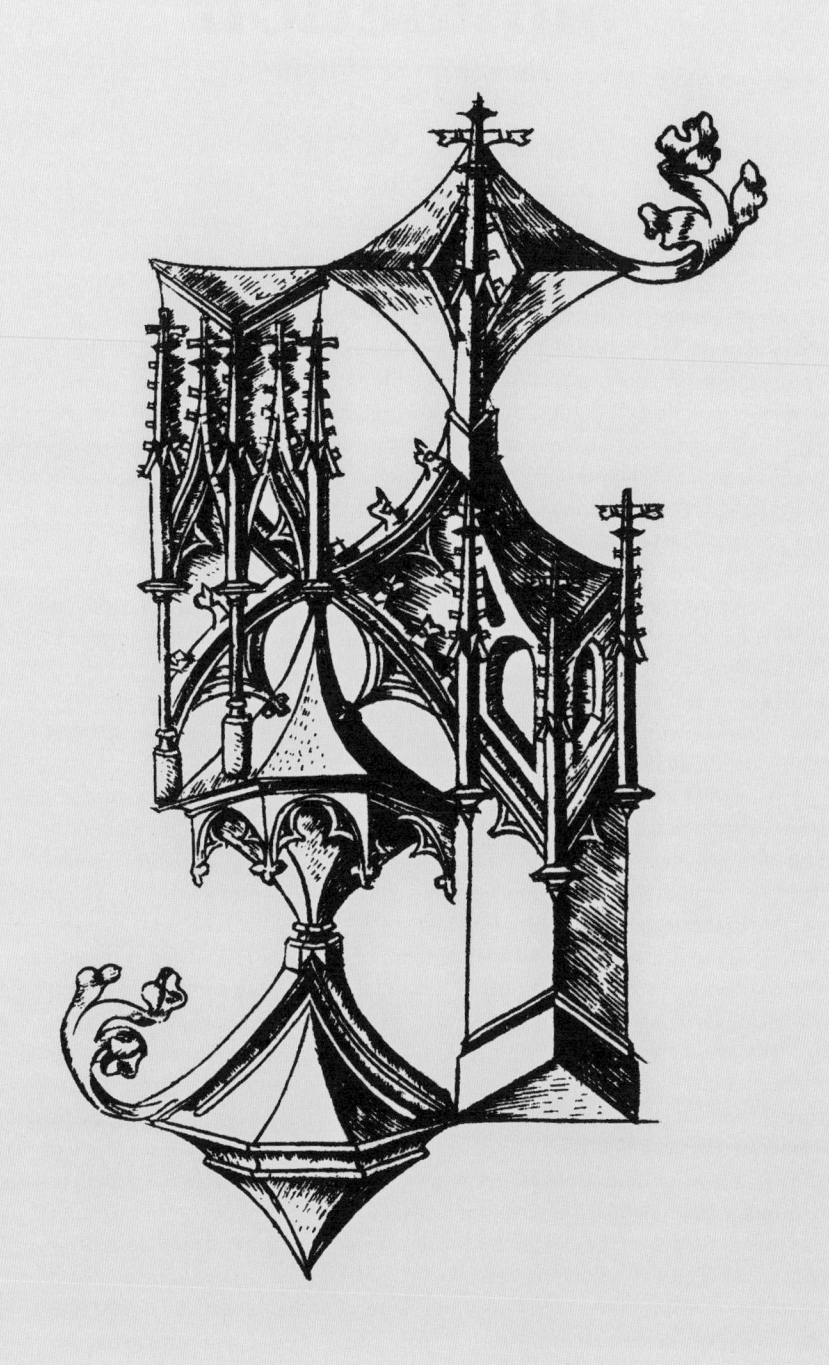

Simulation
Hermann Schlimme

Simulation is a procedure used for analysing complex, dynamic systems. In a simulation, experiments are performed on a model to gain insights into real-life situations. Many different fields apply simulations. They are used for the optimization of technological procedures – for example, testing within design processes, training via flight simulators and for computer games. In 1987 Holger van den Boom observed, 'Unlike the model', simulations are 'not object-oriented but user-oriented'. As Stephan Ott remarked in his editorial in 2019 for the 'Simulation Shifts Design' issue of *Form* magazine, Van den Boom's assertion surprised most designers at that time, but simulation is common practice today.

Ideally, in order to fully comprehend architecture, one should be able to walk freely into and around it. Simulations empower people to have spatial and sequential experiences by being fully immersed in a representation of architecture and moving through it at will. In a performative way, people 'live' architecture and learn about its characteristics. Media used in architectural simulations include photographic sequences, films, CCTV and digital tools. All these media cope well with movement and the space and time dimensions of architecture.

In the digital realm, which is the focus of this essay, simulations are commonly based on digital models and virtual realities, and enable their sequential and four-dimensional exploitation. Simulations are regularly applied in the context of architecture or architectural concepts that do not exist in physical reality. This may happen in the design process, for buildings never realized or realized with major alterations, or for buildings that are lost today or have been significantly modified. The changes to a building over time or throughout the construction process can be visualized through simulation.

The uses of simulation in the field of architecture are countless. In the digital realm, simulation is as old as computer-aided design itself and can be performed through various tools and techniques ranging from the computer screen to full immersion in the CAVE (Cave Automatic Virtual Environment) system. On walks through towns or heritage sites, one may compare the existing spatial situation with a former lost one, which a smartphone app shows simultaneously on screen; an example is the site of the Old Summer Palace in Beijing. Other simulations project sequences of construction phases or particular events from the history of a building on to the corresponding walls, floors and vaults of archaeological sites, and thus enable visitors to explore the historic dimensions of a place, as is the case at the Palazzo Valentini in Rome.

In scholarly contexts, simulations are used to answer specific research questions concerning space and spatiality. The simulation illustrated here was created in 2018–19 and depicts Hans Poelzig's fertilizer production plant, which was realized according to his design in 1909–12 in Luboń, near Poznań in Poland (known as Luban when it was part of Prussia). The creator of the simulation is Christian Uhl, who participated in a graduate history course on Poelzig that I taught in the winter term of 2018/19 at the Technische Universität Berlin.

Hans Poelzig (1869–1936) was one of the most important architects of his generation in Germany. Beginning from a deep understanding of historical building culture, Poelzig updated architectural characteristics of existing building types such as residential buildings and churches, and expressed them in a contemporary way. For the new building types of his era, such as commercial and industrial buildings, he famously generated new, specific expressions developed from the very core of these types, without introducing any architectural ingredients from other contexts. For industrial sites he did not cite, for example, the architectural language of historic palaces. In 1911, at the time of the construction of the plant at Luboń, Poelzig declared in the journal *Der Industriebau*, 'The buildings of most industrial plants inherently necessitate differences in height; the volumes are different in size, there is the chimney, the water tank, the tower-like facilities, which are necessary for a

Stills from the virtual model of Hans Poelzig's fertilizer production plant (1909–12) in Luboń, near Poznań, Poland, by Christian Uhl, student at the Technische Universität Berlin, 2018–19.

lot of factories. This is sufficient to ensure an often impressive rhythm to the whole thing.' Poelzig recognized the characteristic nature of an industrial plant as being this functional composition of volumes, and understood that its architecture had to enhance this; it had to be transformed into a scenographic composition. How did Poelzig manage to accomplish this transformation at the Luboń plant, which hosted a complex, multiphase production process and was accordingly made up of a series of different buildings of diverse character and size?

Several photographs were taken at Luboń by Heinrich Götz and others immediately after the completion of the factory. In the photographs, the composition of volumes is framed and fixed. But only by walking through, with the aid of simulation, are we able to understand how Poelzig managed to transform the functional composition of volumes into an architectonic composition of scenographic quality. The buildings in Luboń are in large part no longer standing, and the remaining ones have been greatly altered. Based on a virtual reality model produced using the Rhinoceros program, a simulation in Unity software was created, in which one could move freely through the site. The simulation shows dozens of significant scenographic compositions of volumes, and demonstrates that Poelzig succeeded in his task of transformation.

In the still image on the upper right, one can see the raw phosphate mill in the centre, flanked by two stepped buildings: the main production building to the far left and the delivery shelter to the right. The whole is framed by a conveyor. Moving on, in the still on the lower right, one now sees the main production building and the mill, which are connected to each other by another conveyor and frame the power station, the lower volume seen in diagonal view. The power station, surmounted by the chimney, centres the group. For the moving spectator, these scenographies dynamically emerge, shift, decompose and freshly recompose. Poelzig's 'rhythm' may be intended as a question of movement. It is something that develops through a timeline and can be experienced through simulation. We learn about Poelzig's intention for the real, original architecture. The example of Poelzig's factory in Luboń shows that simulations are cognitive tools. They allow one to use digital models and virtual reality to answer specific questions about spatial and sequential experience in research and other contexts.

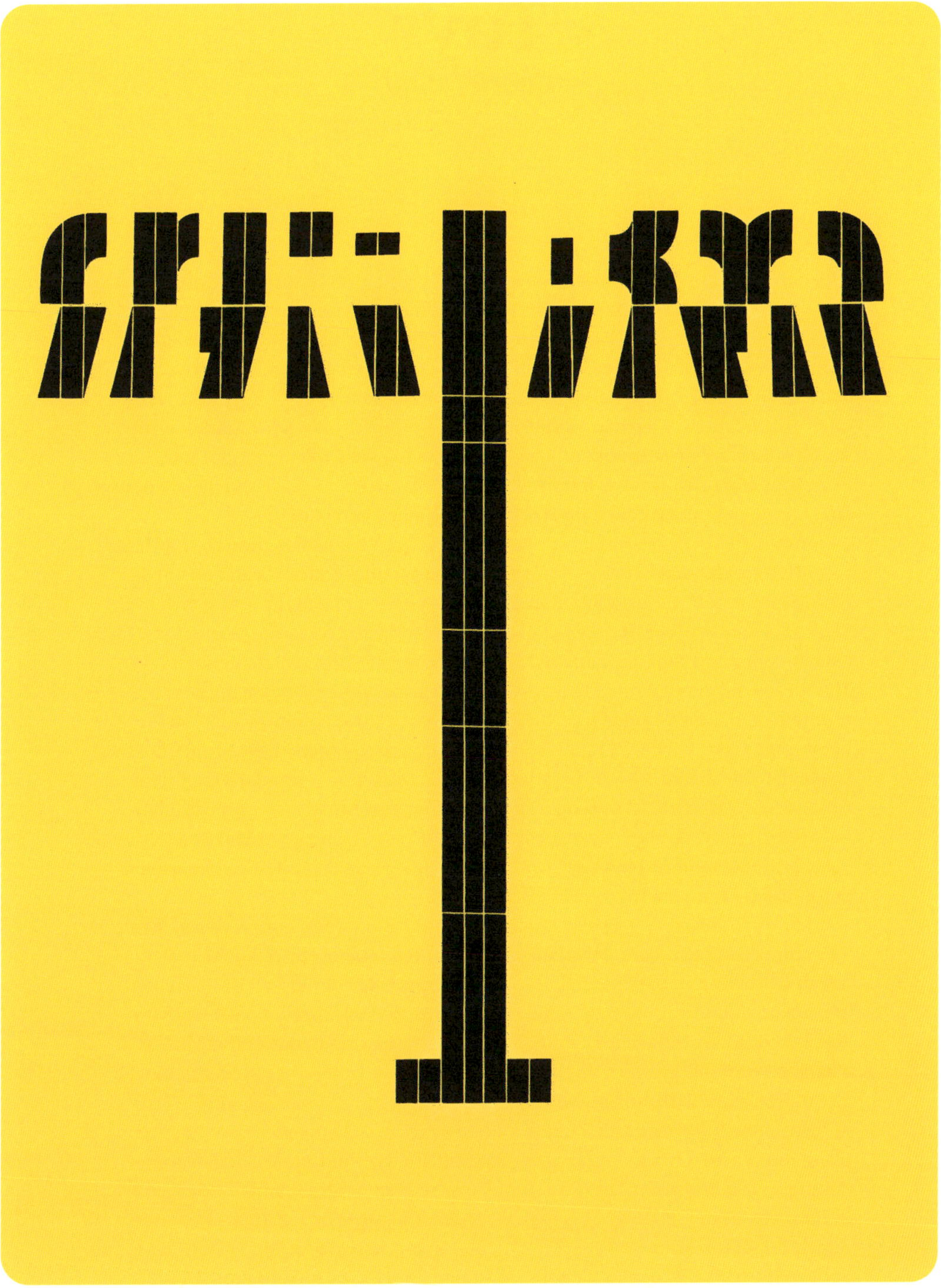

Toys
Charles Hind

Architectural toys were an invention of the late eighteenth century; the earliest mention of building bricks for children was in *Practical Education* (1798) by Maria Edgeworth and Richard Lovell Edgeworth. At first, they were for educational purposes rather than entertainment, and taught children about gravity, physics and spatial relationships. Commercially made building toys first appeared in early nineteenth-century Germany, which dominated the European toy market until the First World War. Subsequently other countries wished to encourage their own industries and provide work for disabled servicemen. The earliest toys were wooden; later common materials included composition, metal and plastic.

Although wooden toys became less popular from the 1930s onwards, they have recently experienced a revival thanks to environmental concerns and nostalgia. Historically, wood was usually left in its natural state, but from the 1840s onwards, engraved, hand-coloured paper was occasionally pasted on to the blocks. Sets usually contained columns and arches as well as square or rectangular blocks. The earliest surviving sets were made in Thuringia, a region of Germany with a long tradition of making wooden toys. Wood was also the most common material for home-made sets. Vacher's Model Bricks were a rare late-nineteenth-century English product, made in Manchester. Each wooden box, the size of a standard English brick, contained wooden bricks one-quarter the size of a real brick, with proportionate halves and quarters. The set was 'designed for the use of Architects and Builders, Teachers and Pupils in Technical Schools, Boys' and Girls' Schools, Kindergartens and as a good Nursery Toy'.

More contemporary toys include KAPLA, a Dutch system first produced in 1987. This comprises identical small planks of pine, in the ratio of 1:3:5, stained in various colours. Gravity and balance hold the pieces in place. The American KEVA Planks of maple are similar. Children are the primary but not sole market: the planks are advertised as therapeutic for soldiers suffering from PTSD, prisoners seeking to establish relationships with their families, and stressed university students, as well as children with ADD and autism.

From the 1870s onwards, children could build more sophisticated structures using composition bricks, made of compressed quartz sand, chalk and linseed oil. For more than fifty years, the most popular were Anchor Stone Building Sets, made in Germany from 1880 by F.A. Richter. With effective advertising, the sets became hugely popular worldwide. The brand name 'Anker', and in English 'Anchor', was applied from 1894, and manufacture continued until 1963. The sets consisted of blocks of many different shapes and sizes (eventually over 1000), stained in three colours to simulate yellow sandstone, red brick and blue slate for roofs. The weight and texture of the blocks were sufficient to hold structures together, and illustrated instruction manuals showed how elaborate constructions could be built. Unusually, to judge by the advertising material, the manufacturer assumed that girls as well as boys would enjoy creating buildings. Architects said to have played with these blocks include Walter Gropius, Frank Lloyd Wright and Richard Buckminster Fuller.

British toymaking, including construction toys, developed dramatically in the 1920s. Lott's Bricks (1918–60) were also made of composition, and they gradually superseded Anchor blocks in the British market. They had cardboard roofs and were accompanied by instruction manuals with designs created by architects such as Arnold Mitchell (1863–1944). They included designs for such topical structures as a war shrine. Variant designs allowing Tudor and other styles were introduced in later years.

An alternative material was artificial stone, epitomized by Brickplayer, launched in 1938 by J.W. Spear & Sons of Enfield. Brickplayer sets included manuals on how to build models 'designed by a firm of chartered architects' and bags of 'cement' that dissolved in water to allow models to be dismantled and the bricks reused. By the time manufacture ended in the early 1960s, the original metal elements for windows and doors had been replaced by plastic.

A box of Minibrix produced in Britain c. 1940.

One of the earliest metal construction toys was Wenebrik, manufactured in 1915–39 by William Bailey of Birmingham and marketed as 'An instructive architectural toy'. The five sets available contained folded painted metal pieces representing bricks and roof tiles, along with windows and hinged doors. Bailey also made Kliptiko, a frame-based toy aimed particularly at boys, while girls were targeted for Wenebrik. Meccano was an earlier system, patented in 1901, that could be used for making architectural structures (particularly the Meccano Erector Set), but was better suited for building engineering models.

Rubber was an uncommon but practical material for construction sets. Minibrix, made in Hampshire by the Premo Rubber Company, were patented in 1935 and manufactured into the 1970s. From the bottom of each brick protruded two nodules that locked into the brick below. First made of card, by 1936 roofs were made of rubber sheets, while windows and doors were printed plastic. Instruction manuals contained designs for buildings drawn up by a local architect, W.A.T. Carter. The idea may have been derived from an American toy called Bild-O-Brik, introduced in early 1934, and was the foundation of many modern systems, including Kiddicraft (1947) and its later derivative, the hugely popular Danish Lego.

Among the earliest plastic construction toys was Bayko, made in Liverpool in 1934–67. The name is derived from Bakelite, one of the world's first commercial plastics, from which many of the parts were made. Bayko had several different sets that could be upgraded inexpensively with 'conversion sets'. The Danish Lego system was first marketed in 1949 and is probably the most popular construction set ever made, with an endlessly inventive stream of additional items appearing on the market. The American Skyline system allowed children to design and build high-rise blocks. Sold in the late 1950s and early '60s, it was made in Chicago by Elgo Plastics.

Many sets these days are designed with adults in mind rather than children. Lego has a series of sets that reproduce important buildings such as Frank Lloyd Wright's Fallingwater, as well as an elaborate 'Architecture Studio' set explicitly aimed at those over sixteen years old. The latter includes a 272-page book with designs by an international group of architects, including SOM of Chicago. Much simpler adult-oriented building blocks are those in the wooden Blockitecture series, designed by the industrial designer James Paulius. With the 'Blockitecture Habitat' set you can build your own version of the iconic Habitat 67 apartments, designed by Moshe Safdie for Expo 67, the World's Fair held in Montreal in 1967.

What all these toys offer is the opportunity for children to use their imaginations to construct in miniature their own environments. In the process, whether consciously or not, they learn about space and structure, balance and planning, knowing that they can always demolish and start again: model-making in its simplest and most enjoyable form.

U

Urban
Patrick Mckeogh

When you think of 'urban', you immediately think of 'city'. But both these short words encompass such complex elements and ideas that once you start to isolate one aspect and move into more detail (something model-makers inevitably find themselves doing), it becomes overwhelming. That is the particular challenge of the urban environment: it's everything. It's your home, your work, your school, your friends, your recreation and everything on your route between them. It's vast amounts of activity and interaction. It's many people, many voices, all experiencing it both as individuals and as a community. The ability to zoom in and out, grappling simultaneously with the macro and micro challenges and opportunities, is essential in helping to shape our urban environment and create better cities.

As model-makers, we are all too familiar with the challenge of maintaining perspective amid a raft of detail. One of the fundamentals of our industry is that we are constrained by scale. In order for the architecture of a building to be understood, it must be modelled at a suitably large scale, which immediately limits our ability to communicate its context. Conversely, the wider we open the lens to offer a greater understanding of the urban environment, the less we can explore the detail of a

New London Architecture's 1:2000 scale model of London, produced by Pipers Model Makers, 2015.

scheme. These may sound like the undesirable limitations of an analogue tool, but architectural models are a reflection of their human creators and how we interact with our world. After all, it is not only model-makers who seek perspective, can't see the wood for the trees or are asked to think outside the box. And before you rush to technology for the answer, spend some time on Google Earth and assess how well the human mind copes with moving back and forth between Street View and Maps.

It is not surprising that the majority of projects for which we produce models lie within an urban environment, as that is where most development takes place. However, that explains only the amount of development, not what drives the demand for models. Anyone looking to develop in a city has to engage with a wide range of stakeholders, from planners, politicians and the community to investors and potential occupiers. Failure to communicate your project effectively and to secure support from each of these diverse groups is the difference between it becoming a reality or yet another design that never gets built. Each group will have their own concerns and expectations, and their ability to interpret technical drawings and reports in order to assuage the former and satisfy the latter will vary greatly. Hence the need for models, which communicate in a language everyone can understand.

The first engagement we typically receive on a project is for a context model. Made up of simple block massing and little architectural detail, these models are simple enough to construct. The opportunity and challenge, however, is to define the genuine context of the scheme. What area will be impacted by the development? To what will the project be responding? The answers to these questions – which determine the size of the area that needs to be modelled – vary from scheme to scheme. The masterplan for the redevelopment of Elephant and Castle in south London, for example, has a far wider impact than an intervention in a nearby row

New London Architecture's interactive model of London helps both professionals and the public better understand their city and how it is changing.

of terraced houses; but with both projects it is still necessary to fully understand the impact. Setting the boundaries for the model actually sets the parameters for all future discussions. From this point on in a project, the scheme will be examined in greater detail and modelled at larger scales; we return to the initial model to check that the latest iterations of the design are still appropriate to the context, but rarely move outside of these boundaries. The model is a distillation of the huge amount of work done by the project team, and helps to simplify and communicate their thinking.

It is an enormous privilege to be a part of this process. It means that, long before construction starts on site and buildings begin to emerge in our cities, we have already built them – in miniature, of course. We are offered a sneak peek of the future and, because the time lag between the model and the completed development is so long, it can be quite surreal to encounter a building in real life that some years ago you were holding in your hand. Stranger still have been the walks around King's Cross, where the early phases of the masterplan have been completed while the rest of the 27-hectare (67-acre) site is still under development. The phased programme has allowed us to walk around the redevelopment over the past decade and watch each of the forty-two buildings we have modelled become a reality – in almost the exact order we constructed the miniature versions!

Perhaps more interestingly, we are also afforded the opportunity to see what might have been, as many of the plans we initially model never come to pass. This is usually because the designs evolve and are superseded by others, but in some cases it is down to economic and political changes. Whenever a new building we worked on is completed, I always take the time to review any other plans we had looked at for the site and imagine the alternative reality. To get a taste of this, I'd recommend looking up Christopher Wren's plans for rebuilding London after the Great Fire of 1666. He envisaged a reconstructed capital full of wide boulevards and grand civic spaces, similar to Paris and Rome. This never came about for the reason that, while Wren was busy trying to convince Charles II to divert funds from the war with the Dutch, enterprising Londoners asserted their property rights and got on with rebuilding on the previous medieval street pattern, so they could continue trading. Try to imagine what London would look like today if Wren had succeeded in convincing both the Crown and the property owners to share his vision. Perhaps he should have invested in a model.

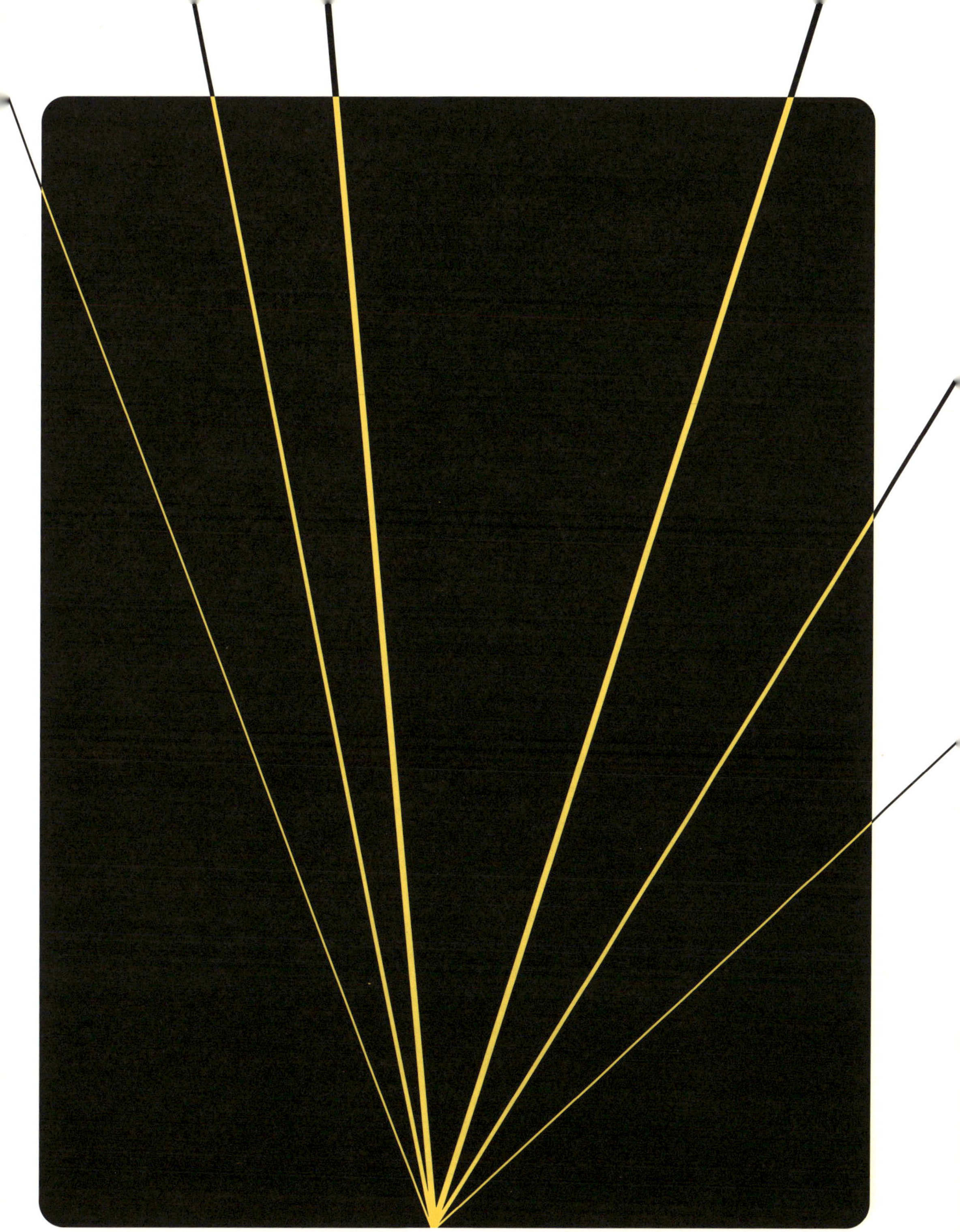

Virtual
ScanLAB Projects

The virtual world is an emulation or simulation of the real. Modern 3D-capturing technologies have enabled us to replicate the real in high-fidelity virtual models to the point that the virtual emulation can often seem more genuine than its physical counterpart. When the virtual and the real worlds are indistinguishable, we start questioning the authenticity of the world around us and whether we are already living in a simulation.

In architectural practice, the virtual plays the important role of materializing a dream, an idea, a concept. CGI virtual models have increased in fidelity and believability in line with Moore's Law (the prediction made in 1965 by Gordon Moore, the co-founder of Intel, that the number of transistors that can fit on a microchip would increase at an exponential rate), and now many previously isolated industries are merging: game design, VFX, architecture and computer science.

In such a mixed-disciplinary context, the virtual model offers us a malleable universe full of possible impossibilities. A virtual version can be perfect, uncanny, accurate to the submillimetre. It can also defy the laws of physics, which state that

Still from ScanLAB's virtual reality point-cloud animation 'Limbo', based on 3D scan data, 2017.

the 'real' must exist within. In this way, the virtual model is able to represent what is invisible to the naked eye.

Ephemeral, atmospheric and hypothetical features of the real world are sometimes tricky to embody in architectural models. A plethora of scenarios can enrich our virtual models of the world. The visual representation of such features is assimilated by the eye as a complex system of errors, potential malfunctions and unexpected results that triggers a new questioning and investigation of our 'real' world and of our cognitive capabilities.

We are beginning to inhabit virtual models at a human scale. How do we absorb, make use of and consume these digital twins? Capturing the real allows us to create our own doppelgänger, but the relationship that we are going to establish and develop with our virtual self is still in its infancy. In part this is due to the mediation of emerging 3D-visualization hardware: virtual reality (VR), augmented reality (AR) and extended reality (XR) devices. These devices act as new sets of physical eyes, altering information, offering 3D experiences and augmenting our perceptions. We are just beginning to learn to live with them.

In the post-Anthropocene era, the virtual will exist not just in screen space; we will live within it. We will no longer be the dominant force constructing our world. Spatial computing (XR) will soon form a new layer of our reality, and its consequences for design practices are yet to be explored.

As we increasingly physically inhabit the virtual world, we will form our own personal memories within it. The open nature of a brand-new world virtually accessible by anyone at any time has implications for the ownership of our newly created memories and the control that we want and need over them. We will be

Still from ScanLAB's virtual reality animation 'Dream Life of Driverless Cars', based on 3D scan data, 2015.

allowed to relive our memories, to visualize them and experience them over and over again in three-dimensional, realistic environments. But the retrieval of these memories will no longer be in the hands of our subconscious minds. What had been until this point an involuntary exercise of the mind might now become automatic and intelligently controlled but prone to interpretive errors. Our selective memories (as we choose to remember events from our own perspective) could forever be re-examined, reinterpreted, reframed, reused. Moreover, the millimetric accuracy of our memory recording could be capable of uncovering previously hidden details and potentially reshape our understanding of past events.

The act of capturing everything quickly and at extreme resolutions locks evidence securely in a digital world to be examined hours, months or even decades later. An example is the development of forensic architecture research and discoveries via the use of 3D-scanning technology. The scanner's ability to document space at meticulous levels of detail far exceeds what is humanly possible with a tape measure and sketchbook. The consequent three-dimensional visualization allows the past to be reconsidered, rethought and rediscovered, bringing history into a more proximate layer of time.

Scan data and 3D visualizations of virtual spaces have the unique ability to capture architecture and our world over time and space. The architectural model in its virtual form is now able to hold and store information and details belonging to a very precise moment in history. The encapsulated point in time can contain universal information (such as permanent aspects of the physical world, including size and volume) that stays constant in any analysis of the past or future, as well as details of the particular moment (such as weather and light conditions and the movement of people), which can all vary.

The morphology of our urban landscape also offers rich ground for the encapsulation of physical and chronological data. This data has the power to inform our wandering through cities as well as our future means of transportation. Driverless cars are the most compelling example in their assimilation of our cities as a massive 3D architectural model. As driverless cars navigate the streets, slowing for speed bumps and stopping in traffic, they automatically map our world while at the same time extrapolating useful references for our own safe wandering. The urban virtual model is now simultaneously created and deployed by autonomous vehicles in a perpetually referenced and updated version of our cities.

The physical world is no longer alone; it is cloaked in a virtual version of past, future and present. One is slow to reform but has permanence, monumentality and tactility. The other is flexible and transient, and it has the potential to be a more powerful force for the future than humankind. As designers and early adopters, we have an opportunity to inform the relationship between the two.

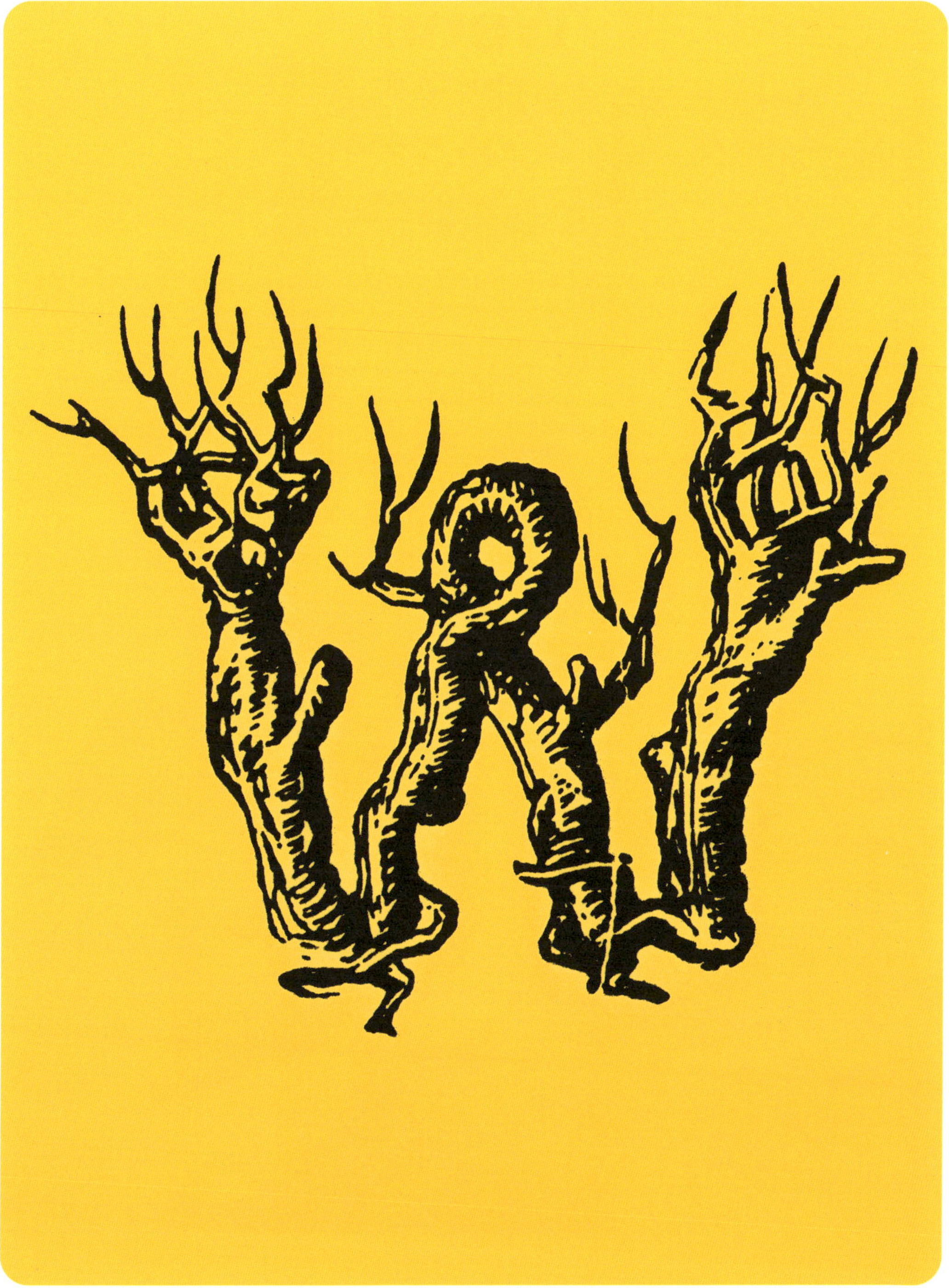

Wood
Barnabas Calder

In the 1950s, Denys Lasdun (1914–2001) began to emerge as an independent architect after the break-up of Tecton, the practice in which he had been a partner. In early post-Tecton jobs, Lasdun's assistants helped him test design ideas through alternative options, in line-drawn perspective, often schematically shaded, through which Lasdun would judge the most aesthetically satisfactory solution. Using the two-dimensional medium of pencil on tracing paper to investigate his proposals in three dimensions was effective, but labour-intensive and slow.

During the planning process for the headquarters of the Royal Institution of Chartered Surveyors in Westminster, an unexecuted and three-dimensionally

Denys Lasdun with his model-maker Philip Wood, examining the model of the library extension for the School of Oriental and African Studies (SOAS), London, 1970.

Model, probably from 1965, for Lasdun's partially realized National Theatre and Opera House, South Bank, London, comprising moveable wooden blocks to test the massing and composition of the overall design.

complex project, Lasdun met Philip Wood, at that time a model-maker for the London County Council Architects Department. Wood was so good at his craft that Lasdun poached him from the council and employed him as a full-time model-maker at his practice.

Wood's presence changed the office's design methodology. What previously had been done with laboursome sequences of drawn options was increasingly accomplished by Lasdun playing with balsa wood, then asking Wood to shave a chamfer off a corner or to cut a different slab plan. Devastatingly for historians, these models were destroyed even in the process of their creation, and none survives. Instead, from around 1964, the record left by Lasdun's design process tends to be patchy, surviving only when designs were presented to clients or 'drawn up' for internal use and discussion within the office.

History's loss was architecture's gain: through working models, Lasdun could simultaneously explore functional disposition and form. He could monitor the aesthetic effects of each decision as it was made. Philip Wood recalls Lasdun on more than one occasion taking a model into a park close to the office with a black cloth draped over the model and his head, in order to see how light would fall into an interior.

Even before Wood joined Denys Lasdun & Partners, models, and photographs of models, were becoming an indispensable tool for presenting Lasdun's designs to clients and in publications. Initially, following the example set by Tecton, Lasdun relied heavily on drawings for the demonstration of design ideas and to communicate varied and complex practical and formal decisions. By the early 1960s, however, in his work for Fitzwilliam Hall in Cambridge, he refused to provide presentation drawings for the fundraising literature, insisting instead on the use of photographs of the presentation model. From this point onwards, Lasdun used model photographs as the main publication images of almost all his schemes, until the completed building could itself be photographed.

These models were almost always made of balsa. In a photograph that Lasdun submitted successfully for his Royal Academy membership in 1991 (p. 51), we see a heap of models involved in the design process for the National Theatre on the south bank of the Thames. The photograph shows Lasdun's method of designing with sheets of balsa cut to profiles whose edge parapets would form the external expression of the building, and whose internal penetrations would make the building's foyer spaces and vertical circulation. In the case of the National Theatre, the balsa models were worked on for five years before the final designs were produced in a matter of months from a series of finalized balsa models. Even during the production of working drawings, important details were tested in balsa, sometimes up to 1:1 scale. One might argue that the composition of the building as slabs and faceted towers was directly influenced by the planar materiality of balsa-wood sheet in the model-making process.

The building's predominant surface treatment, too, seems to owe something to balsa photographed in black and white. Board-marked, exposed *in situ* concrete recalls the grain of the wooden models. The boards were offset by fractions of an inch, allowing the texture of wood to exist not only close up but also from greater distances. The grain is exhaustively emphasized by the use of rough-sawn wood for the shuttering, and each board was used only twice to avoid the grain becoming dulled by residual cement. The concrete itself is obsessively perfect in the heightened woodiness of its surface.

Once Lasdun turned to designing with models, the models themselves became an important design source. The medium itself became in some respects an idealized form of the building. A key creative tension in the finished buildings is that between miniaturized balsa perfection and beautifully crafted concrete reality.

Tab. XVIII.

X-ray
Lisa Nash

The process of conserving an architectural model made of diverse materials often necessitates the use of different specialisms and skills because of the complexities encountered. A model may require knowledge from experts outside the field of conservation, particularly if it has moveable parts or sections, or incorporates electrical and mechanical elements that could lead to physical or chemical changes. Therefore, there are many ways a conservator looks at an object, from the naked eye alone to the use of more intricate scientific tools.

The deterioration of an architectural model can be affected by several factors: the use of different materials, often of low grade; weakening adhesives; fluctuating temperature and humidity within storage or display conditions; display methods; transportation; poor handling due to weight or size; and inadequate packing. Common types of damage that models suffer include breaks, adhesive failure, material distortions, cracking, pest activity, mould and structural collapse.

Areas of decline in condition can be made visible through the use of specialist tools, and in the case of a three-dimensional model such tools can be useful to help determine potential areas of weakness or structural vulnerability. Since many architectural models are made of a combination of materials that each react differently to environmental conditions, it is important to understand the problems in order to plan for long-term care.

The fundamental way of looking at an object is by using the naked eye to make immediate observations on the object's condition.

Raking light is a bright oblique light that reveals more details than ambient natural light, and can highlight to a greater degree distortions, breaks, sheen and surface textures.

Ultraviolet (UV) light has wavelengths in the electromagnetic spectrum between 10 nanometres and 400 nanometres, and is invisible to the naked eye. Some materials absorb and re-emit energy from UV radiation in a longer wavelength as visible light. When UV light is used for examination at around 360 nanometres, outer-layer surface imperfections that might otherwise be difficult to see, such as historic repairs, varnishes, mould and faded inks, become evident as UV-induced visible fluorescence. Inspection under UV light can provide evidence as to how an object was constructed, and assist in the identification of materials, and thus can aid the dating of the object.

Infrared light is at the red end of the electromagnetic spectrum, with wavelengths ranging between 750 nanometres and 1200 nanometres, and is generally invisible to the naked eye. Infrared has longer wavelengths than visible light, and these have the ability to penetrate an object below the surface. Infrared imaging is the recording of the variable absorption and reflectance of infrared light by an object. The use of this process enhances the contrast between materials and/or features, and therefore can assist in material identification. Infrared light is often used to look for alterations and carbon-based underdrawings, as the carbon becomes opaque under IR imaging.

X-ray is an electromagnetic wave of high energy and very short wavelength. An image of the internal structure of an object can be produced by X-rays passing through it and being absorbed to different degrees by different materials, depending on their thickness. X-rays help make visible the internal structure of an object, and therefore can be used to identify breaks, joins, inlays of different materials and internal sections of enclosed objects, and to illustrate and aid our understanding of the structural composition.

In architectural models, higher density materials such as metal absorb more X-ray waves than lower density materials such as wood and paper; some plastics cannot be detected.

For museums, this method of analysis is advantageous for artefacts because it is non-invasive and uses non-destructive diagnostic techniques that do not require the removal of any original material samples for testing.

The model of a house at Oxshott, Surrey (c. 1920; RIBA Collection, London), by Reginald C. Fry, was constructed using barbotine, a modelling clay, set into a wooden frame. From the X-ray image, we can see that internally the model is heavily pinned with metal nails, which essentially held the clay in place while it was setting. X-ray imagery informs us that the cracking and lifting damage to the barbotine is substantial, and extends right the way through the model's structure.

The imagery provides evidence that the model was executed in sections, which were attached together to create the components of the main part of the model, the cottage. We can determine that twenty-one nails were used to secure the various clay sections of the cottage, while three larger screws secured the base of the model to the wooden

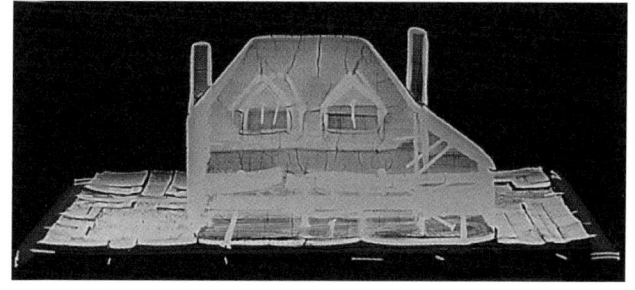

Model of a house at Oxshott, Surrey (c. 1920), by Reginald C. Fry. The X-ray shows extensive use of metal nails in the construction process and reveals damage to the modelling clay through cracking.

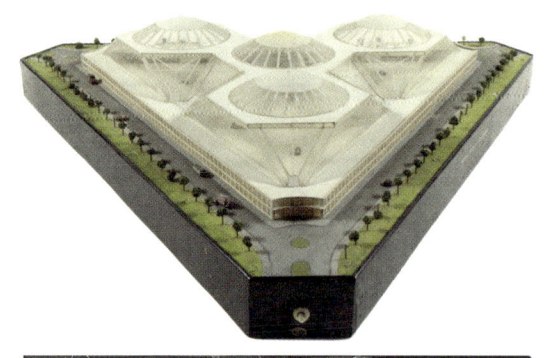

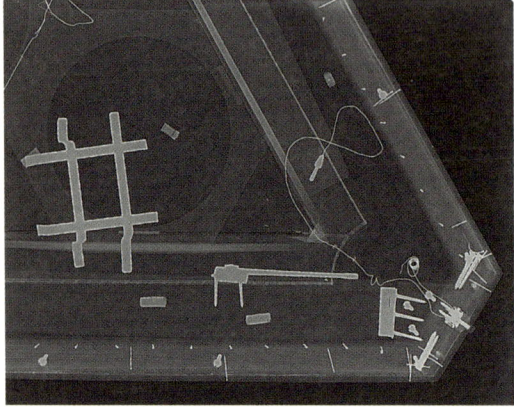

Model of an unrealized scheme for an aircraft maintenance hangar (c. 1950) at London Airport by Sir Owen Williams. The X-ray reveals the internal workings of the lights.

frame. A further twenty-three nails were used around the base of the frame to pin the modelling clay in position.

X-rays show that the areas that were pinned initially for structural purposes have increased the cracking of the modelling clay. To prevent future cracking, the model is housed in an environmentally controlled storage facility, where the temperature and, crucially, the relative humidity are kept within set parameters.

The model of a proposed but unbuilt hexagonal-triangular-shaped scheme for an aircraft maintenance hangar at London Airport (now Heathrow) by Sir Owen Williams was made by E.J and A.T. Bradford in about 1950 (RIBA Collection). It was constructed of mixed media: plastics, metals, foam, card and plaster. The use of so many materials is problematic for the conservator, because they respond differently to environmental conditions and therefore will deteriorate at different rates.

X-ray images confirm our suspicions that the model had originally been fitted with an internal lighting feature that has since been dismantled. The imagery helps us to determine how the lighting was fitted and how it illuminated the main area of the model. The metal aircraft and cars inside the hangar are clearly visible in the X-rays, but cannot be seen as easily from outside the model because of the ageing and yellowing discoloration of the plastic elements used to indicate the glass of the building.

The model has built-in wooden legs that are riveted to fold into the base, the original intention being that it could be displayed free-standing. The legs are not visible when they are tucked inside the base and they are now quite loose, so the inclusion of X-ray imagery in our condition reports informs collection staff how best to move the model safely without the rivets and legs incurring any damage.

X-ray imagery is an invaluable tool for the conservation management of architectural models. Such images reveal the construction techniques of the model-maker and offer the conservator a greater understanding of a model's constituent materials and how they interact with one another; they therefore are of great help in deciding a model's optimal environment and treatment, and in ensuring its conservation and preservation.

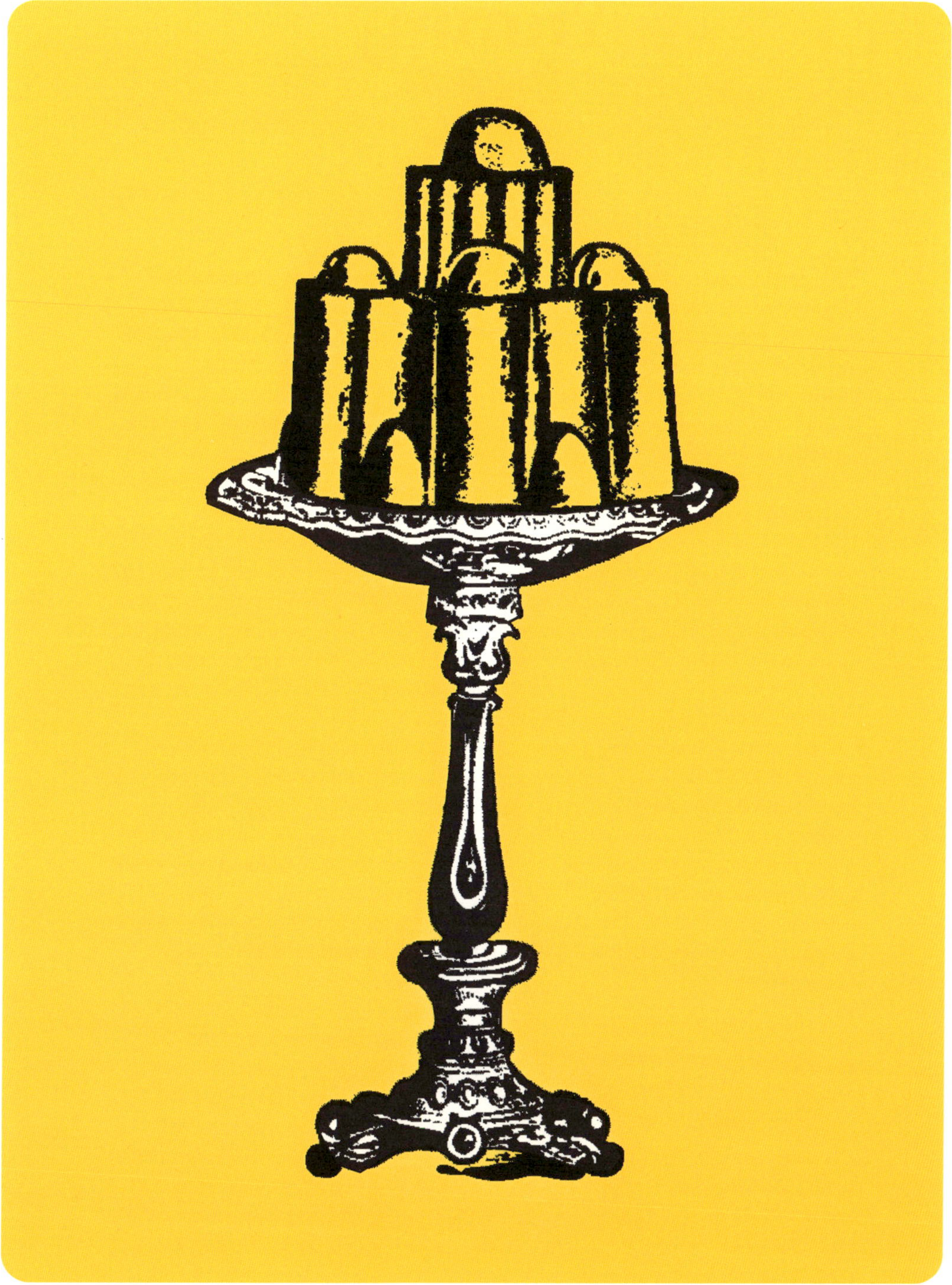

Yummy
Mark Morris

Edible architectural models are rare but glorious treats featuring in literature, film and the occasional holiday. In Marcel Proust's *In Search of Lost Time* (1913–27), Albertine describes her obsession with ices made in moulds of various architectural forms: '[W]henever I take one, temples, churches, obelisks, rocks, it is like a picturesque geography which I first look at and then convert its raspberry or vanilla monuments into coolness in my gullet.' Recalling similar model desserts served at the Ritz, she gushes, 'I set my lips to work to destroy, pillar by pillar, those Venetian churches of a porphyry that is made with strawberries, and send what's left over crashing down upon the worshippers.'

It seems a strange pleasure, eating architectural representations, but if architecture can be experienced by the other senses – visually, tactilely, acoustically (the echoing tread of steps along a church aisle) and even olfactorily (the dusty scent of an attic triggering a sense of nostalgia) – why should the sense of taste be barred? To the extent that models are meant to represent buildings that might manifest, an edible one underlines the reality of the thing. As James Thurber argued, 'Seeing is deceiving. It's eating that's believing.'

For those of us who have not been lucky enough to sup on a Proustian model ice, we can recall the delight of nibbling some inconspicuous corner of a gingerbread house. Historically, gingerbread was supposed to be enjoyed at Easter and Christmas and made only by members of the gingerbread guild. A finely decorated miniature house was the acknowledged masterpiece of a professional gingerbread-maker. 'Hansel and Gretel', according to the Brothers Grimm, featured a house with walls made merely of bread. But this is transformed into chocolate cream and gingerbread, with candies for architectural details, in Engelbert Humperdinck's opera of 1893:

> The roof is all covered with Turkish delight,
> the windows with lustre of sugar are white;
> and on all the gables the raisins invite,
> and think! all around is a gingerbread hedge!

As its name implies, gingerbread was originally spiced bread or cake, a holiday indulgence when spices were luxury goods. Ginger, used as a preservative, is only one of several spices – among them nutmeg, allspice, cinnamon, cloves, aniseed and ground pepper – that might be included in a gingerbread recipe. It is the Old French term for ginger itself, *gingebras*, that migrated to English as the word for the cake.

Nuremberg's honeyed *Lebkuchen* straddle the cake/cookie divide, and it is out of that fourteenth-century culinary tradition that denser dough arrived and formed horses, hearts and, finally, houses. Architecture mimicking gingerbread in a generic sense can be seen in certain late nineteenth-century house designs noted for their fancy carpentry details, referred to as Gingerbread.

A satire of 'Hansel and Gretel' in *The Simpsons* – in the Halloween episode 'Treehouse of Horror XI', first shown in 2000 – includes a candy-as-architecture joke in a scene in which Homer tries to rescue Bart and Lisa from a gingerbread house, but forgets his purpose once he decides to eat his way in:

Lisa: Father! I knew you'd rescue us!
Homer: Oh, rescue you, stuff myself with candy, it's all good!
Witch: Oh, that's a load-bearing candy cane! You clumsy oaf!

The 'King of Chefs and Chef of Kings', Marie-Antoine Carême, made his career in the early nineteenth century out of *pièces montées*, claiming, 'The fine arts are five in number, namely: painting, sculpture, poetry, music and architecture, the principal branch of the latter being pastry.' As in the case of gingerbread houses, *pièces montées* are meant to be principally decorative and secondarily edible. Nevertheless,

Zaha Hadid cutting a cake model of her proposal for The Peak Leisure Club, Hong Kong, at the private view of the exhibition Zaha Hadid: Planetary Architecture Two *at the Architectural Association, London, 1983.*

Carême's were explicitly architectural models: castles, temples, churches, pagodas of fondant, nougat and marzipan. Peter Greenaway's 1987 film *The Belly of an Architect* plays up the Carême-style edible model in a memorable scene. The architect protagonist is presented with a cake in the shape of Étienne-Louis Boullée's design for a cenotaph to Sir Isaac Newton. Its dome mimics both the architect's rotund belly and that of his pregnant wife. The cake scene takes place in front of the Pantheon in Rome, another great dome.

In 1983 Zaha Hadid famously celebrated her competition design for The Peak Leisure Club in Kowloon, Hong Kong, with a magnificent chocolate-cake model served in the library of the Architectural Association. Although unbuilt beyond the buttercream version, The Peak is credited by the Museum of Modern Art in New York as being a 'pivotal' project in Hadid's career. Its siting was significant, the carving and reconfiguring of the rocky slope intended for the private health club offering 'a man-made geology', according to the architect. So the edible model included an edible hillside of cake. The celebration around it was joyously communal, with everyone tasting Hadid's success.

The artist Liz Hickok turned to another foodstuff for her breakthrough project, *San Francisco in Jell-O*, in which the city is cast in coloured gelatin. 'I drew inspiration for this project from my immediate surroundings in San Francisco, where the geological uncertainties of the landscape evoke uncanny parallels with the gelatinous material', she says. The model buildings and landmarks wiggle on command as the table can effect a miniature earthquake. Hickok's photographs capture these wiggly moments: 'These site-specific Jell-O installations introduce the viewer to a more physical experience involving smell, movement and the desire to taste.' John Ruskin wrote of such desire during his tour of Italy in 1852:

> There is a strong instinct in me, which I cannot analyse, to draw and describe the things I love – not for reputation, nor for the good of others, nor for my own advantage, but a sort of instinct, like that for eating and drinking. I should like to draw all St Mark's and all this Verona stone by stone, to eat it all up into my mind, touch by touch.

This is more than Thurber's believability test; Ruskin longs to consume architecture as a means to fully understand it. He wants to tap every sense and, Albertine-like, to come to know Venetian churches through imagined eating. The edible model indulges such ambition, letting the least likely of senses in on architectural appreciation.

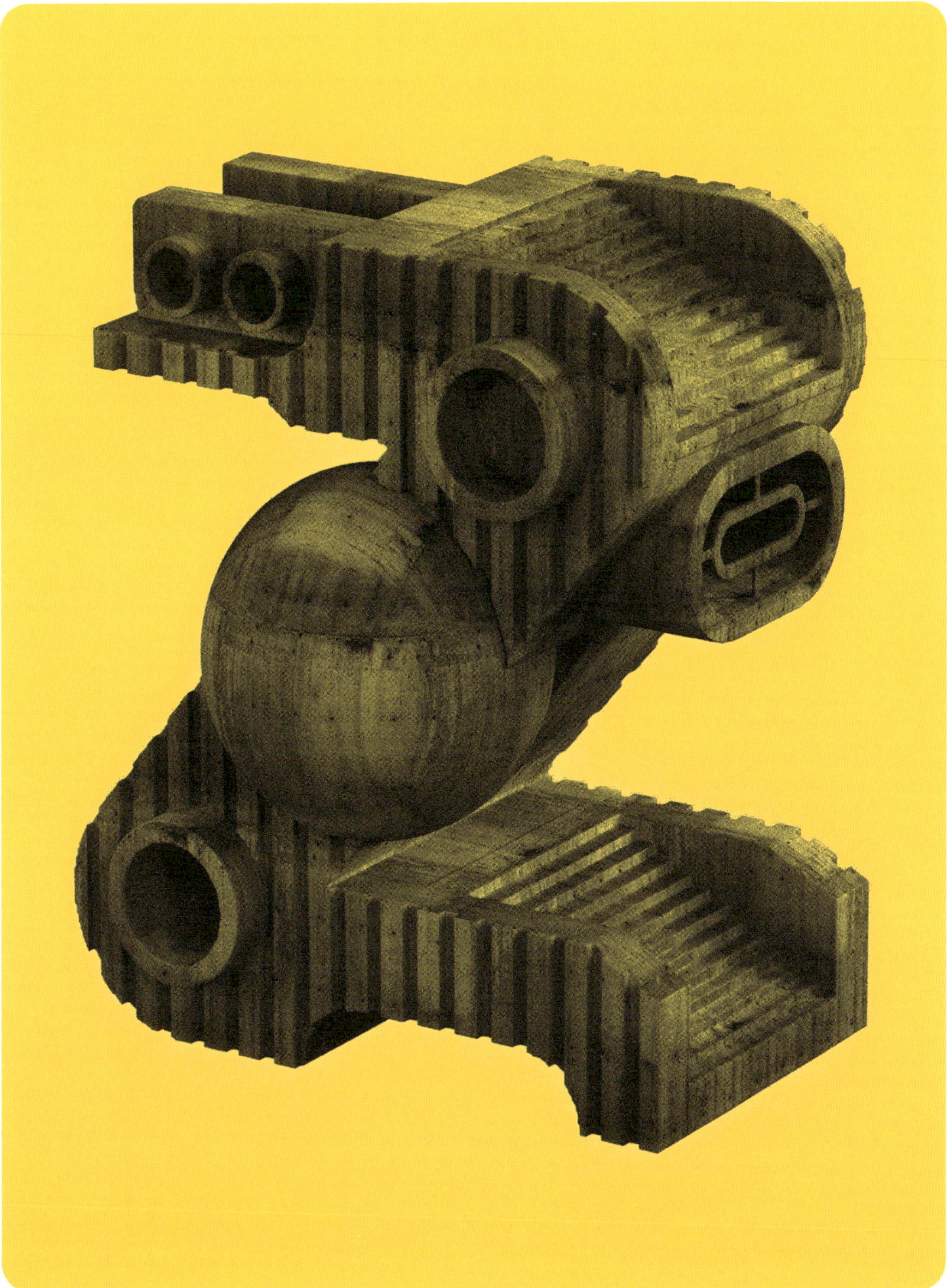

Zoom
Davide Deriu

Photography has played a significant role in the production and reproduction of architectural models over the past century. While early examples of 'model photographs' can be traced back to the nineteenth century, it was in the 1920s that this class of images became widespread. Two phenomena converged at that historical juncture: at the same time as modern architecture became aligned with the culture of mass media, model-making made a major comeback after a period of decline. Photography contributed to this revival by mediating the image of miniatures alongside that of full-scale buildings. Although pictures of models were widely disseminated in the interwar architectural press, only recently has this imagery been appraised as a key aspect of the Modernist visual repertoire.

The resurgence of model-making after the First World War has been ascribed to a variety of economic, practical and aesthetic reasons linked to the rise of Modernism, but it was also bound up with emerging techniques of representation. It can be argued, paraphrasing Walter Benjamin, that to an ever-greater degree the architectural model reproduced became the architectural model *designed for reproducibility*. A fundamental paradox underlies this historical shift: by reducing the materiality of models to a flat surface, photography produced a realistic representation of virtual environments. While the model owed much of its renewed popularity to its inherent objecthood, which allowed designers to communicate ideas effectively to clients and the public in solid form, concurrently this three-dimensional medium was incorporated in the visual space of the camera and gained broad currency as a two-dimensional image. The relationship between photography and model-making is historically defined by this intermedial process.

The proliferation of model photographs in the early twentieth century was fostered by the increasing circulation of architectural books and magazines. The significance of this phenomenon is evidenced by the number of influential projects that became widely known through this class of images, including Ludwig Mies van der Rohe's glass skyscraper design for Berlin (1922) and Le Corbusier's Plan Voisin for Paris (1925). While these and other now-classic models gained exposure through public exhibitions, it was their photographs that forever inscribed them in the architectural imagination. Even when design ideas were built – as, for example, in the case of Le Corbusier's Maison Citrohan in 1927 – model views acquired an iconic status that often surpassed that of the actual buildings. Through the careful choice of framing and lighting, photographers transfigured the physical objects into images that would travel across time as well as space.

Right in the heyday of the Modern Movement, the versatility of the photographic image contributed to the renewed popularity of models in design education and professional practice alike. European avant-garde schools that emerged after the First World War, notably the Bauhaus in Weimar and Dessau and the Vkhutemas in Moscow, adopted model-making in their curricula while also embracing photography for the representation of study models. Meanwhile, growing numbers of architects took advantage of the possibilities offered by scale models and their images. A miniature could be photographed from a variety of angles, enabling architects to visualize different scenarios in ways that were more expedient and economic than rendered drawing. Furthermore, sequential views were used to show patterns of spatial distribution, moveable elements or particular methods of construction and assemblage. Whether as a single image or in a series, the model photograph became a standard feature of architectural representation.

The diverse uses of this imagery reflected a variety of design strategies. At one end of the spectrum was the abstract representation of design concepts viewed in isolation. Those pictures, favoured by avant-garde magazines, staged models as if they were floating in a realm of ideas – pristine objects devoid of any context. At the other end lay a rather different approach that drew on the hyperrealism of photography. This method is exemplified by so-called 'double photography', a technique that consists of combining a model view with a picture of the intended site, the montage being then photographed to simulate a building in its prospective context. The American architect Harvey Wiley Corbett was among the pioneers of this method in the 1920s.

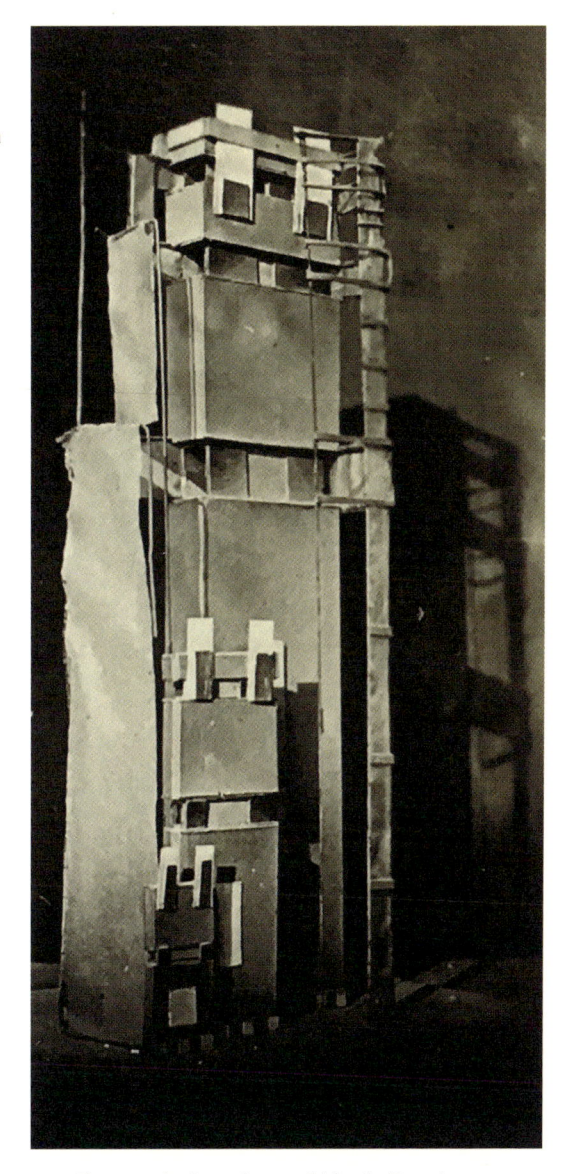

Photograph of a student model for the 'Space' course at the Vkhutemas (Higher State Artistic Technical Studios), Moscow, Russia, 1922–23.

This hyperrealistic imagery reached the peak of illusionism after the Second World War, when the introduction of sophisticated model-making techniques and materials made it possible to combine, almost seamlessly, pictures of the engineered models with views of sites usually taken from street level or from the air. Among the most striking results were those created in Chicago by Hedrich-Blessing photographers, whose crisp montages helped to popularize the sleek American buildings designed by Mies van der Rohe in the 1950s and '60s. These studio compositions can be regarded as precursors of the computer-generated renderings that were to become a staple of the digital age. In the 1970s, before the arrival of digitalization, attempts were made to achieve more convincing representations of miniatures through the use of video technology. The experiments in model video simulation led by John M. Anderson at the Mackintosh School of Architecture at the Glasgow School of Art, in particular, were aimed at bridging the so-called 'Gulliver Gap' – that is, the discrepancy between human and miniature scales that is perceived when one looks at a model.

While these and other uses of camera-based media sought to visualize the world of miniatures in the most verisimilar ways, at the same time a backlash against realism was staged by such theoretically minded architects as Peter Eisenman, who instigated the *Idea as Model* exhibition in New York in 1976. In different forms, this impetus to reclaim the model's autonomy as a means of architectural expression lives on today. While digital media and 3D-printing technologies have widely expanded the range of three-dimensional representations, they have not yet rendered obsolete the practices of hand-making and photographing models. Scores of architectural students and practitioners continue to exploit the creative potential of this intermedial process.

In parallel, this potential has also been explored by visual artists interested in the ambiguity of scalar perception. The photographic works of James Casebere, Thomas Demand and Naoya Hatakeyama are particularly provocative in this respect. They invite us to reconsider the notion of the model itself by interrogating *what* we see when we look at a model photograph: a peculiar class of image, involving the representation of a representation, which still exerts a powerful hold on our imagination.

Select Bibliography

GENERAL

Architecture and Its Image: Four Centuries of Architectural Representation – Works from the Collection of the Canadian Centre for Architecture, exhib. cat., ed. Eve Blau and Edward Kaufman, Montreal, Canadian Centre for Architecture, May–August 1989

Das Architekturmodell: Werkzeug, Fetisch, kleine Utopie/The Architectural Model: Tool, Fetish, Small Utopia, exhib. cat., ed. Oliver Elser and Peter Cachola Schmal, Frankfurt am Main, Deutsches Architekturmuseum, May–September 2012

Briggs, Martin S., 'Architectural Models – I', *The Burlington Magazine for Connoisseurs*, vol. 54, no. 313, April 1929, pp. 174–75, 178–81, 183

——, 'Architectural Models – II', *The Burlington Magazine for Connoisseurs*, vol. 54, no. 314, May 1929, pp. 245–47, 250–52

Carroll, Peter, 'On Models', *Building Material*, no. 15, Autumn 2006, pp. 16–17

de Chadarevian, Soraya and Nick Hopwood (eds.), *Models: The Third Dimension of Science*, Stanford, Calif. (Stanford University Press) 2004

Fankhänel, Teresa, *The Architectural Models of Theodore Conrad: The 'Miniature Boom' of Mid-Century Modernism*, London (Bloomsbury) 2021

Frémy, Anne, *Modell*, Cologne (Walther König) 2002

Frommel, Sabine, and Raphaël Tassin (eds.), *Les Maquettes d'architecture: Fonction et évolution d'un instrument de conception et de réalisation*, Paris/Rome (Picard/ Campisano) 2015

Idea as Model: 22 Architects 1976/1980, ed. Kenneth Frampton and Silvia Kolbowski, New York (Rizzoli) 1981; catalogue of an exhibition held at the Institute for Architecture and Urban Studies, 1976

Lending, Mari, and Mari Hvattum (eds.), *Modelling Time: The Permanent Collection 1925–2014*, Oslo (Torpedo Press) 2014

La Maquette: Un outil au service du projet architectural – Actes du colloque qui s'est tenu les 20–21 mai 2011 à la Cité de l'Architecture et du Patrimoine, Paris (Éditions des Cendres) 2015

Marble Halls: Drawings and Models for Victorian Secular Buildings, exhib. cat. by John Physick and Michael Darby, London, Victoria and Albert Museum, August–October 1973

Mindrup, Matthew, *The Architectural Model: Histories of the Miniature and the Prototype, the Exemplar and the Muse*, Cambridge, Mass. (MIT Press) 2019

Moon, Karen, *Modeling Messages: The Architect and the Model*, New York (Monacelli Press) 2005

Morris, Mark, *Models: Architecture and the Miniature*, Chichester (Wiley) 2006

Porter, Tom, and John Neale, *Architectural Supermodels: Physical Design Simulation*, Oxford (Architectural Press) 2000

Smith, Albert C., *Architectural Model as Machine: A New View of Models from Antiquity to the Present Day*, Oxford (Architectural Press) 2004

Stavrić, Milena, Predrag Šiđanin and Bojan Tepavčević, *Architectural Scale Models in the Digital Age: Design, Representation and Manufacturing*, Vienna and New York (Springer) 2013

Valeriani, Simona, 'Models and Knowledge Production: Mechanical Arts, Natural Philosophy, and the State in Early Modern Europe', in *Encyclopedia of Early Modern Philosophy and the Sciences*, ed. Dana Jalobeanu and Charles T. Wolfe, Cham (Springer) 2020, https://doi.org/10.1007/978-3-319-20791-9_257-1 (accessed April 2021)

Wells, Matthew J., 'Architectural Models and the Professional Practice of the Architect, 1834–1916', PhD thesis, Royal College of Art/Victoria and Albert Museum, London, 2019

Wendler, Reinhard, *Das Modell zwischen Kunst und Wissenschaft*, Paderborn (Wilhelm Fink) 2013

Wilton-Ely, John, 'The Architectural Model', *The Architectural Review*, vol. 142, no. 845, July 1967, pp. 26–32

CASE STUDIES

Berteloot, Mathieu, and Véronique Patteeuw, 'Form/Formless: Peter Zumthor's Models', *OASE*, no. 91, 2013, pp. 83–92

Carile, Maria Cristina, 'Buildings in Their Patrons' Hands? The Multiform Function of Small Size Models between Byzantium and Transcaucasia', *kunsttexte.de*, no. 3, 2014

Centofanti, Mario, Stefano Brusaporci and Vittorio Lucchese, 'Architectural Heritage and 3D Models', in *Computational Modeling of Objects Presented in Images: Fundamentals, Methods and Applications*, ed. Paolo Di Giamberdino et al., Cham (Springer) 2014, pp. 31–49

Cuisset, Geneviève, 'Jean-Pierre et François Fouquet, artistes modeleurs', *Gazette des beaux-arts*, 6th series, vol. 115, 1990, pp. 227–40

Gerrewey, Christophe van, '"What Are Men to Rocks and Mountains?" The Architectural Models of OMA/ Rem Koolhaas', *OASE*, no. 84, 2011, pp. 31–36

Jeffery, Paul, 'The Commissioners' Models for the Fifty New Churches: Problems of Identity and

Attribution', *The Georgian Group Journal*, vol. 5, 1995, pp. 81–96, 135–36

Knox, Tim, 'Ecclesiastical Models', *RIBA Journal*, vol. 99, no. 8, August 1992, pp. 30–33

——, 'Cockerell's Model for Langton: A House for the "Dorsetshire Nimrod"', *The Georgian Group Journal*, vol. 3, 1993, pp. 62–67

Kockel, Valentin, 'Plaster Models and Plaster Casts of Classical Architecture and Its Decoration', in *Plaster Casts: Making, Collecting and Displaying from Classical Antiquity to the Present*, ed. Rune Frederiksen and Eckart Marchand, Berlin and New York (De Gruyter) 2010, pp. 419–33

Leslie, Fiona, 'Inside Outside: Changing Attitudes Towards Architectural Models in the Museums at South Kensington', *Architectural History*, vol. 47, 2004, pp. 159–200

Lillie, Amanda, and Mauro Mussolin, 'The Wooden Models of Palazzo Strozzi as Flexible Instruments in the Design Process', in *Giuliano da Sangallo*, ed. Amedeo Belluzzi, Caroline Elam and Francesco Paolo Fiore, Milan (Officina Libraria) 2017, pp. 210–28

Millon, Hank, A., 'Models in Renaissance Architecture', in *The Renaissance from Brunelleschi to Michelangelo: The Representation of Architecture*, ed. Hank A. Millon and Vittorio Magnago Lampugnani, London (Thames & Hudson) 1994, pp. 19–74

Morris, Mark, 'Worlds Collide: Reality to Model to Reality', in *Camera Constructs: Photography, Architecture and the Modern City*, ed. Andrew Higgott and Timothy Wray, Farnham (Ashgate) 2012, pp. 179–94

Patteeuw, Véronique, 'Miniature Temptations: A Conversation with CCA Curator Howard Shubert on Collecting and Exhibiting Architectural Models', *OASE*, no. 84, 2011, pp. 123–27

Richardson, Margaret, 'Model Architecture: Sir John Soane's Collection of Architectural Models', *Country Life*, vol. 183, no. 38, 21 September 1989, pp. 224–27

Tatarinova, Irina, 'Architectural Models at the St Petersburg Academy of Fine Art', *Journal of the History of Collections*, vol. 18, no. 1, June 2006, pp. 27–39

Teerds, Hans, and Job Floris, 'On Models and Images: An Interview with Adam Caruso', *OASE*, no. 84, 2011, pp. 128–33

Tschudi, Victor Plahte, 'Plaster Empires: Italo Gismondi's Model of Rome', *Journal of the Society of Architectural Historians*, vol. 71, no. 3, September 2012, pp. 386–403

Valeriani, Simona, 'Three-dimensional Models as "in-between-objects": The Creation of in-between Knowledge in Early Modern Architectural Practice', *History of Technology*, vol. 31, 2012, pp. 26–46

Weaver, Thomas, 'Model-Maker Grimm', *AA Files*, no. 73, 2016, pp. 94–100

Wells, Matthew J., 'Relations and Reflections to the Eye and Understanding: Architectural Models and the Rebuilding of the Royal Exchange, 1839–44', *Architectural History*, vol. 60, 2017, pp. 219–41

Williams, Matthew, 'Lady Bute's Bedroom, Castell Coch: A Rediscovered Architectural Model', *Architectural History*, vol. 46, 2003, pp. 269–76

Wilton-Ely, John, 'The Architectural Model: English Baroque', *Apollo*, vol. 88, no. 80, October 1968, pp. 250–59

——, 'The Architectural Models of Sir John Soane: A Catalogue', *Architectural History*, vol. 12, 1969, pp. 5–38, 81–101

——, 'The Role of Models in Church Design', *Country Life Annual*, 1969, pp. 76–77, 79

Yorke, James, 'Tiny Temples of Mr Nash', *Country Life*, vol. 195, no. 6, 8 February 2001, pp. 66–67

Cork

Dorey, Helen, 'Sir John Soane's Model Room', *Perspecta: Grand Tour*, vol. 41, 2008, pp. 46, 26, 92–93, 170–71

Elsner, John, 'A Collector's Model of Desire: The House and Museum of Sir John Soane', in *The Cultures of Collecting*, ed. John Elsner and Roger Cardinal, London (Reaktion) 1994, pp. 155–76

Gercke, Peter, and Nina Zimmermann-Elseify (eds.), *Antike Bauten: Korkmodelle von Antonio Chichi, 1777–1782*, Kassel (Staatliche Kunstsammlungen Kassel) 2001

Gillespie, Richard, 'Richard Du Bourg's "Classical Exhibition", 1775–1819', *Journal of the History of Collections*, vol. 29, no. 2, July 2017, pp. 251–69

——, 'The Rise and Fall of Cork Model Collections in Britain', *Architectural History*, vol. 60, 2017, pp. 117–46

Grand Tour: The Lure of Italy in the Eighteenth Century, exhib. cat., ed. Andrew Wilton and Ilaria Bignamini, London, Tate Gallery, October 1996–January 1997; Rome, Palazzo delle Esposizioni, February–April 1997

Kockel, Valentin, 'Rom über die Alpen tragen: Korkmodelle antiker Architektur im 18. und 19. Jahrhundert', in *Rom über die Alpen tragen. Fürsten sammeln antike Architektur: Die Aschaffenburger Korkmodelle*, ed. Werner Helmberger and Valentin Kockel, Landshut (Arcos) 1993, pp. 11–31

——, *Phelloplastica: Modelli in sughero dell'architettura antica nel XVIII secolo nella collezione di Gustavo III di Svezia*, Stockholm (Istituto Svedese di Studi Classici a Roma) 1998

——, 'Models of Pompeii from the Eighteenth Century to the "Grand Plastico": The Three-Dimensional Documentation of Ancient Ruins', in *Pompeii and Europe, 1748–1943*, exhib. cat., ed. Massimo Osanna, Maria Teresa Caracciolo and Luigi Gallo, Naples, Museo Archeologico Nazionale di Napoli, May–November 2015, pp. 255–75

Digital

Archaeology of the Digital: Peter Eisenman, Frank Gehry, Chuck Hoberman, Shoei Yoh, exhib. cat., ed. Greg Lynn, Montreal, Canadian Centre for Architecture, May–October 2013

Carpo, Mario, *The Second Digital Turn: Design Beyond Intelligence*, Cambridge, Mass. (MIT Press) 2017

Frazer, John, *An Evolutionary Architecture: Themes VII*, London (Architectural Association) 1995

Frei Otto: Thinking by Modeling, exhib. cat., ed. Georg Vrachliotis *et al.*,

Zentrum für Kunst und Medien Karlsruhe, November 2016–March 2017

Gershenfeld, Neil, 'How to Make Almost Anything: The Digital Fabrication Revolution', *Foreign Affairs*, vol. 91, no. 6, November/December 2012, pp. 43–57

Exhibition

The Architect's Studio: Norman Foster, exhib. cat., ed. Michael Juul Holm, Humlebæk, Louisiana Museum of Modern Art, September–December 2001

Foster Associates: Six Architectural Projects 1975–1985, exhib. cat., Norwich, Sainsbury Centre for Visual Arts, University of East Anglia, June–September 1985

Jenkins, David (ed.), *On Foster ... Foster On*, Munich and London (Prestel) 2000

New Architecture: Foster, Rogers, Stirling, exhib. cat. by Deyan Sudjic, London, Royal Academy of Arts, October–December 1986

Film

Ball, Joseph A., 'Theory of Mechanical Miniatures in Cinematography', *Transactions of the Society of Motion Picture Engineers*, no. 18, 1924, pp. 119–26

Heindl, Gabu, and Drehli Robnik, 'Maßstab und Macht', in *Das Architekturmodell: Werkzeug, Fetisch, kleine Utopie/The Architectural Model: Tool, Fetish, Small Utopia*, exhib. cat., ed. Oliver Elser and Peter Cachola Schmal, Frankfurt am Main, Deutsches Architekturmuseum, May–September 2012, pp. 57–59

Higley, Sarah L., 'A Taste for Shrinking: Movie Miniatures and the Unreal City', *Camera Obscura*, vol. 16, no. 2 (47), 1 September 2001, pp. 1–35

Jordanova, Ludmilla, 'Material Models as Visual Culture', in *Models: The Third Dimension of Science*, ed. Soraya de Chadarevian and Nick Hopwood, Stanford, Calif. (Stanford University Press) 2004, pp. 443–51

Schönberger, Angela, 'Architekturmodelle zwischen Illusion und Simulation', in *Simulation und Wirklichkeit*, ed. Angela Schönberger, Cologne (DuMont) 1988, pp. 41–55

Vana, Gerhard, *Metropolis: Modell und Mimesis*, Berlin (Gebrüder Mann) 2001

Waltenspül, Sarine, 'Das Maß, das Monströse und die Miniatur: Körper und Skalierung im Film', in *Kleine Medien: Kulturtheoretische Lektüren*, ed. Oliver Ruf and Uta Schaffers, Würzburg (Königshausen & Neumann) 2019, pp. 193–211

Gypsum

'The Architectural Courts, South Kensington Museum: The Trajan Column and the Portico de la Gloria, Santiago de Compostela', *The Builder*, vol. 31, no. 1600, 4 October 1873, p. 789

Frederiksen, Rune, and Eckart Marchand (eds.), *Plaster Casts: Making, Collecting and Displaying from Classical Antiquity to the Present*, Berlin and New York (De Gruyter) 2010

Lending, Mari, *Plaster Monuments: Architecture and the Power of Reproduction*, Princeton, NJ, and Oxford (Princeton University Press) 2017

Hand

Luckhardt, Wassili, 'Vom Entwerfen', *Stadtbaukunst alter und neuer Zeit*, vol. 2, no. 11, 1921, pp. 169–70

Mies van der Rohe, Ludwig, untitled, *Frühlicht*, no. 4, 1922, pp. 122–24

Junk

'The Klotz Tapes: The Making of Postmodernism', special issue, *Arch+*, no. 216, 2014

Lynch, Kevin, *Wasting Away*, ed. Michael Southworth, San Francisco (Sierra Club Books) 1990

Strasser, Susan, *Waste and Want: A Social History of Trash*, New York (Metropolitan Books) 1999

Landscape

Bürgi, Andreas (ed.), *Europa Miniature: Die kulturelle Bedeutung des Reliefs, 16.–21. Jahrhundert/Il significato culturale dei rilievi plastici, XVI–XXI secolo*, Zurich (Verlag Neue Zürcher Zeitung) 2007

Corvisier, André (ed.), *Actes du colloque international sur les plans-reliefs au passé et au présent, les 23, 24, 25 avril 1990 en l'Hôtel National des Invalides*, Paris (SEDES) 1993

Faucherre, Nicolas, Guillaume Monsaingeon and Antoine de Roux, *Les Plans en relief des places du roy*, rev. edn, Paris (Éditions du patrimoine/Biro Éditeur) 2007

Raymond, Florence, and Dominique Tourte (eds.), *Le Regard souverain: Les plans-reliefs dans les collections du Palais des Beaux-Arts de Lille*, Lille (Invenit) 2019

Warmoes, Isabelle, *Le Musée des Plans-Reliefs*, Paris (Éditions du patrimoine) 2019

Narrative

Goren, Haim, '"Undoubtedly, the best connoisseur of Jerusalem in our times": Conrad Schick as "Palästina-Wissenschaftler"', in *Palaestina exploranda: Studien zur Erforschung Palästinas im 19. und 20. Jahrhundert anläßlich des 125jährigen Bestehens des Deutschen Vereins zur Erforschung Palästinas*, ed. Ulrich Hübner, Wiesbaden (Harrassowitz) 2006, pp. 105–28

——, and Rehav Rubin, 'Conrad Schick's Models of Jerusalem and Its Monuments', *Palestine Exploration Quarterly*, vol. 128, no. 2, 1996, pp. 103–24

In Statu Quo: Structures of Negotiation, exhib. cat., ed. Ifat Finkelman *et al.*, Venice Biennale, 16th International Architecture Exhibition, Israeli Pavilion, May–November 2018

Röhl, Constanze, 'Conrad Schick: Leben und Werk eines deutschen Architekten im Jerusalem des 19. Jahrhunderts', in *Migration und Baukultur: Transformation des Bauens durch individuelle und kollektive Einwanderung*, ed. Heiderose Kilper, Basel (Birkhäuser) 2019, pp. 147–62

One to One

Morgan, Mary S., 'Learning from Models', in *Models as Mediators: Perspectives on Natural and Social Science*, ed. Mary S. Morgan and Margaret Morrison, Cambridge and New York (Cambridge University Press) 1999, pp. 347–88

Paper

Overpelt, Laura, '"Accommodate the Stories to the Spaces and Not the Spaces to the Stories": Plans, Models and Drawings for Giorgio Vasari's Decorations in the Palazzo Vecchio in Florence', in *The Creation of Space: Proceedings of the Conference (Istituto Universitario Olandese di Storia dell'Arte, 10–11 June 2016)*, ed. Lex Bosman, Leiden (Brill) forthcoming

Richardson, T.A., *The Art of Architectural Modelling in Paper*, London (John Weale) 1859

Santucci, Giovanni, 'Federico Brandani's Paper Model for the Chapel of the Dukes of Urbino at Loreto', *The Burlington Magazine*, vol. 156, no. 1330, January 2014, pp. 4–11

——, '*Come hanno fatto molti*: The Use of Architectural Paper Models in Early Modern Italy', in *The Creation of Space: Proceedings of the Conference (Istituto Universitario Olandese di Storia dell'Arte, 10–11 June 2016)*, ed. Lex Bosman, Leiden (Brill) forthcoming

——, 'The Use of Architectural Paper Models in Medici Florence', in *Building with Paper: The Materiality of Renaissance Architectural Drawings*, ed. Dario Donetti and Cara Rachele, Turnhout (Brepols) forthcoming

Quick

Pallasmaa, Juhani, *The Eyes of the Skin: Architecture and the Senses*, London (Academy Editions) 1996

Representation

'Aéroport de New-York-Idlewild: Bâtiment de la T.W.A.', *L'Architecture d'aujourd'hui*, no. 77, 1958, pp. 10–13

Arnheim, Rudolf, *Visual Thinking*, Berkeley, Los Angeles and London (University of California Press) 1969

Black, Max, *Models and Metaphors: Studies in Language and Philosophy*, Ithaca, NY (Cornell University Press) 1962

Borcherdt, Helmut, 'Planung des TWA-Flughafengebäudes in New York: Bericht eines ehemaligen Mitarbeiters von Eero Saarinen', *Baukunst und Werkform*, May 1960, pp. 256–63

Harrison, Andrew, *Making and Thinking: A Study of Intelligent Activities*, Hassocks, Sussex (Harvester Press) 1978

Latour, Bruno, *Pandora's Hope: Essays on the Reality of Science Studies*, Cambridge, Mass., and London (Harvard University Press) 1999

Polanyi, Michael, *The Tacit Dimension*, Chicago (University of Chicago Press) 1966

Ryle, Gilbert, *The Concept of Mind*, Chicago (University of Chicago Press) 1949

Simulation

Dodd, Samuel, 'Televising Architecture: Spatial Simulations and the "Scanning Finger"', *Art Journal*, vol. 78, no. 1, 2019, pp. 18–29

Gleininger, Andrea, and Georg Vrachliotis (eds.), *Simulation: Presentation Technique and Cognitive Method*, Basel (Birkhäuser) 2008

Heffley, Divya Rao, 'Vision in Motion: Architectural Space Time Notation and Urban Design, 1950–1970', PhD thesis, Brown University, 2011

Picon, Antoine, *Digital Culture in Architecture: An Introduction for the Design Professions*, Basel (Birkhäuser) 2010

Poelzig, Hans, 'Der neuzeitliche Fabrikbau', *Der Industriebau*, vol. 2, no. 5, 1911, pp. 100–106

'Simulation Shifts Design', special issue, *Form*, no. 282, March/April 2019

Uhl, Christian, 'Industriebau: Chemische Fabrik', in *Die humanistischen Grundlagen der modernen Architektur: Schinkel. Poelzig, Koldewey*, exhib. cat., ed. Jörg H. Gleiter, Hermann Schlimme and Thekla Schulz-Brize, Institut für Architektur, Technische Universität Berlin, 2019, pp. 84–87

Virtual

Glynn, Ruairi, and Bob Sheil, *Fabricate: Making Digital Architecture*, London (UCL Press) 2011

Manaugh, Geoff (ed.), *Landscape Futures: Instruments, Devices and Architectural Inventions*, Barcelona (Actar) 2013

Wood

Calder, Barnabas, 'Medium or Message? Uses of Design and Presentation Models by Denys Lasdun and Partners', in *Proceedings of the 2nd International Conference of the European Architectural History Network*, ed. Hilde Heynen and Janina Gosseye, Brussels (Koninklijke Vlaamse Academie van België voor Wetenschappen en Kunsten) 2012, pp. 452–56

Zoom

Cámara y modelo: Fotografía de maquetas de arquitectura en España, 1925–1970/Modelling for the Camera: Photography of Architectural Models in Spain, 1925–1970, exhib. cat., ed. Iñaki Bergera, Madrid, Museo ICO, February–May 2017

Deriu, Davide, 'Transforming Ideas into Pictures: Model Photography and Modern Architecture', in *Camera Constructs: Photography, Architecture and the Modern City*, ed. Andrew Higgott and Timothy Wray, Farnham (Ashgate) 2012, pp. 159–78

Moon, Karen, *Modeling Messages: The Architect and the Model*, New York (Monacelli Press) 2005; see especially Chapter 3, 'A Question of Scale'

Sachsse, Rolf, 'A Short History of Architectural Model Photography', in *Das Architekturmodell: Werkzeug, Fetisch, kleine Utopie/ The Architectural Model: Tool, Fetish, Small Utopia*, exhib. cat., ed. Oliver Elser and Peter Cachola Schmal, Frankfurt am Main, Deutsches Architekturmuseum, May–September 2012, pp. 23–28

Biographies

EDITORS

Dr Teresa Fankhänel is a Curator at the Architekturmuseum der Technischen Universität, Munich, and the author of *The Architectural Models of Theodore Conrad: The 'Miniature Boom' of Mid-Century Modernism* (2021).

Dr Olivia Horsfall Turner, FSA, is Senior Curator of Designs at the Victoria and Albert Museum (V&A), London, and the V&A's Lead Curator for the V&A + RIBA Architecture Partnership. She is responsible for the V&A's collection of architectural designs, including models.

Dr Simona Valeriani is Senior Tutor on the V&A/Royal College of Art History of Design Postgraduate Programme. A historian of architecture and technology, she has a long-standing interest in architectural models, and has published widely on the topic.

Dr Matthew Wells is a Lecturer at the Institute for the History and Theory of Architecture (GTA), ETH Zurich. His doctoral thesis, 'Architectural Models and the Professional Practice of the Architect, 1834–1916', won the Theodor Fischer Award in 2019 and is in preparation for publication.

CONTRIBUTORS

Roz Barr founded Roz Barr Architects in 2010. Her award-winning practice is currently involved in projects in London, Scotland, Spain and New York. She has taught at the Architectural Association, the Bartlett School of Architecture at University College London, and Kingston School of Art.

Dr Barnabas Calder is a historian of architecture and energy at the University of Liverpool. He is the author of *Raw Concrete: The Beauty of Brutalism* (2016) and *Architecture: From Prehistory to Climate Emergency* (2021).

Spencer de Grey is Head of Design at Foster + Partners, having joined the practice in 1973. He is Visiting Professor of Design at the University of Cambridge and a Royal Academician.

Dr Davide Deriu is a Reader in Architectural History and Theory at the University of Westminster. His main area of research lies at the intersection between architecture and visual culture, with a focus on the twentieth century.

Helen Dorey, MBE, FSA, is Deputy Director and Inspectress of Sir John Soane's Museum, London. She has worked on the authentic restoration of Soane's house for more than thirty years, and oversaw the reinstatement of his iconic architectural Model Room in 2016.

Biba Dow and **Alun Jones** established Dow Jones Architects in 2000. Their wide-ranging body of work has won numerous awards and been published internationally. The practice has developed a reputation for making carefully crafted contemporary architecture in complex heritage settings.

Oliver Elser is a Curator at the Deutsches Architekturmuseum in Frankfurt am Main and the co-founder of the Center for Critical Studies in Architecture.

Ulrike Fauerbach is Professor of the History of Architecture and Construction at the Ostbayerische Technische Hochschule Regensburg. She studied Egyptology, holds a doctoral degree in building archaeology, and has published on pharaonic architecture and epistemic history, among other topics.

Martin Hartung is a doctoral fellow at the GTA, ETH Zurich. His research focuses on architectural representations in interdisciplinary and institutional contexts.

Charles Hind, FSA, is Chief Curator and H.J. Heinz Curator of Drawings at the Royal Institute of British Architects (RIBA), London.

As a historian, writer and exhibition curator, he focuses mainly on British architecture from 1700 to 1950.

Mari Lending is a Professor of Architectural History at the Oslo School of Architecture and Design. Among her most recent publications is *Plaster Monuments: Architecture and the Power of Reproduction* (2017).

Dr Ralf Liptau is an architectural historian and has worked at the Universität der Künste Berlin and the Technische Universität, Vienna. His doctoral thesis analysed the role of models in the design process during the twentieth century.

Patrick Mckeogh is Managing Director of Pipers Model Makers. Founded in 1977, the company is a world leader in architectural model-making, helping developers, architects and governments around the globe to bring their plans to life.

Nikos Magouliotis studied architecture and architectural history in Athens and Oslo. He is currently a doctoral fellow at the GTA, ETH Zurich. His writings have featured in *ARCH+*, *Future Anterior*, *Architectural Histories* and *The Journal of Architecture*.

Angel Fernando Lara Moreira is Head of Digital Prototyping at the Architectural Association, London, where he has overseen the introduction of digital fabrication to the curriculum through material experimentation and 1:1 testing.

Mary S. Morgan is the Albert O. Hirschman Professor of History and Philosophy of Economics at the London School of Economics and the author of *The World in the Model: How Economists Work and Think* (2012).

Dr Mark Morris is Head of Teaching and Learning at the Architectural Association. His research focuses on questions of visual representation in the context of the history of architectural education.

Lisa Nash is the Senior Conservator at the Royal Institute of British Architects, where she is responsible for the conservation, preservation, storage and safe display of the RIBA's model collection – one of the largest and most significant in the world.

Vanessa Norwood is a curator, writer and editor. Creative Director of the Building Centre, London, she was co-curator of the British Pavilion, *Venice Takeaway*, at the Venice Biennale, 13th International Architecture Exhibition in 2012, and has led projects for clients including the Albanian government, the British Council and the Wellcome Collection.

Rawden Pettitt is an Associate Director at the London-based architects Stanton Williams and has overseen many of the studio's landmark cultural and civic projects.

George Rome Innes holds a master's degree in art history from Birkbeck, University of London, and has had a long career researching, restoring and making models. His clients include the V&A, Sir John Soane's Museum and other national collections.

Dr Giovanni Santucci is a research fellow in art history at the Università di Pisa. He specializes in the history of architecture and collecting architectural drawings of the early modern period.

ScanLAB Projects is a pioneering creative practice, half art studio, half research laboratory, led by the artists/architects/technologists Matthew Shaw and William Trossell. ScanLAB digitizes the world using 3D scanning, transforming temporary moments and spaces into permanent experiences, images and film.

Hermann Schlimme is Professor and Chair of History of Architecture and Urbanism at the Technische Universität Berlin and co-editor of *Construction History: International Journal of the Construction History Society*.

Dr Sarine Waltenspül is a postdoctoral researcher at the Zürcher Hochschule der Künste, Switzerland. Her scholarship focuses on media, science and architecture.

Isabelle Warmoes is a historian and Deputy Director of the Musée des Plans-Reliefs, Paris. Her research is devoted to the history of fortification and military architecture from the seventeenth to the nineteenth century, including military engineers, cartography and *plans-reliefs*.

Acknowledgements

The origin of this book lies in an international research network, 'Architectural Models in Context: Creativity, Skill and Spectacle', funded by the UK Arts and Humanities Research Council (AHRC), initiated by Simona Valeriani and Olivia Horsfall Turner, and hosted by the Victoria and Albert Museum between 2017 and 2019. We would therefore like to thank the core institutional partners of the network: the V&A, the Royal Institute of British Architects, the Architectural Association, the Architekturmuseum der Technischen Universität, Munich, the MAP Laboratory (CNRS), Sir John Soane's Museum and the Sorbonne, as well as the core network team: Niamh Bhalla, Edward Bottoms, Livio De Luca, Helen Dorey, Sabine Frommel, Charles Hind, Andres Lepik, Mark Morris, Lisa Nash, Vanessa Norwood and Fiona Orsini. We would also like to thank the participants in the network workshops for the ways in which they knowingly, or unknowingly, helped to fuel this project; in London: Charlotte Anstis, Roz Barr, Eleanor Gawne, David Lund, Patrick Mckeogh, Angel Fernando Lara Moreira, Mary Morgan, Jo Norman, Suzie Pugh, Kent Rawlinson and Frances Sands; in Paris: Corinne Bélier, Émilien Cristia, Valentina De Santi, Olivier Delarozière, Chloé Demonet, Kévin Jacquot, Valérie Nègre, Christophe Niedziocha, Émilie d'Orgeix, Hermann Schlimme and Isabelle Warmoes; in Munich: Dieter Cöllen, Oliver Elser, Anton Heine, Amandus Sattler, Lothar Schacke, Anja Schmidt, Kevin Graf Schumacher and Georg Vrachliotis.

The resulting tome is published to coincide with *Shaping Space – Architectural Models Revealed* at the Building Centre, London – a free exhibition and programme of events arising from a collaboration between the V&A and the Building Centre, and supported by the AHRC through Follow-on Funding for Impact and Engagement. We are grateful to our colleagues at the Building Centre, especially Vanessa Norwood, Creative Director, for making the exhibition possible. We warmly thank our contributing authors, who have generously given their time and expertise. Numerous institutions and individuals have been of assistance in sourcing the images included here; we particularly thank the team at Drawing Matter, Nathan Emery at Sir John Soane's Museum and Jonathan Makepeace at the RIBA. We would also like to express our appreciation to Sam Jacob for permission to include an initial letter from his Half-Timbered Alphabet. This publication would not have been possible without the generosity of our sponsors, to whom we are exceedingly grateful: the V&A + RIBA Architecture Partnership, the AHRC, the Built Environment Trust, the Drawing Matter Trust, ETH Zurich, Foster + Partners and Pipers Model Makers. We are indebted to Nicola Bailey, Claire Chandler and Hugh Merrell for their vision, imagination and attention to detail in realizing the volume that you hold in your hands.

V&A + RIBA Architecture Partnership

UKRI Arts and Humanities Research Council

BUILT ENVIRONMENT TRUST
SUPPORTS PEOPLE TO
BUILD A BETTER WORLD

ETH Zürich
Department of Architecture
DARCH *gta*
Institute for the History and Theory of Architecture

Foster + Partners

Alphabet Credits

A (p. 13): From Antonio Basoli, *Alfabeto pittorico*, Bologna (V. Marchi) 1839. © Victoria and Albert Museum, London.

B (p. 17): From Half-Timbered Alphabet by Sam Jacob, 1990. © Sam Jacob.

C (p. 21): Design for a letter 'C' (or Cyrillic 'S') by Iakov Georgievich Chernikhov, *c.* 1940. DMC 2864, © Drawing Matter Collections.

D (p. 25): From Foundry Plek, a dot-matrix typeface designed by The Foundry and based on a 5 × 9 grid system, *c.* 1990s.

E (p. 29): Illuminated letter by Maximilien Vox, introducing the 'Caractères éclairés' section in *Spécimen général des Fonderies Deberny et Peignot*, vol. 2, Paris 1926.

F (p. 33): Graphic by Nicola Bailey, composed of filmstrips.

G (p. 37): Detail of an early twentieth-century plaster cast taken from Trajan's Column, Rome (113 CE). REPRO.6036, © Victoria and Albert Museum, London.

H (p. 41): From Index Initials, Second Series, an alphabet reproduced in Julian Rothenstein and Mel Gooding (eds.), *130 Alphabets and Other Signs*, London (Thames & Hudson) 1993, originally published by Redstone Press in 1991.

I (p. 45): Detail of a drawing made between 1810 and 1815 for Sir John Soane's Royal Academy lectures of a design by John Thorpe of *c.* 1603 for a house in the shape of his initials, I.T. (The distinction between the letters 'I' and 'J' in the Roman alphabet was not fully established until the seventeenth century.) 74/1/1, Courtesy of the Trustees of Sir John Soane's Museum, London, © Sir John Soane's Museum. Photo: Ardon Bar-Hama.

J (p. 49): Graphic by Nicola Bailey, composed of woodblock letters.

K (p. 53): Graphic by Nicola Bailey, composed of pieces from the free-form architectural modelling system Arckit.

L (p. 57): From L.E.M. Jones, *The Landscape Alphabet*, printed by Charles Joseph Hullmandel, *c.* 1830. © Victoria and Albert Museum, London.

M (p. 61): Ornamented letter from a Masonic alphabet by Louis John Pouchée, 1820s. Courtesy of St Bride Library.

N (p. 65): From the *Gothique composée* alphabet in Jean Midolle, *Spécimen des écritures modernes ...*, Strasbourg (Emile Simon fils) 1834–35.

O (p. 69): From Johannes Lencker, *Perspectiva literaria*, Nuremberg (Paul Kauffmann) 1596. RB 282799 (detail), The Huntington Library, San Marino, California.

P (p. 73): From an alphabet composed of letters cut from squares of folded paper, reproduced in Pedro J. Lemos, *The Art Teacher: A Compendium of Ideas, Suggestions and Methods for the Art Education of the Child ...*, London (Batsford) 1931.

Q (p. 77): From Éclair, a typeface designed by Maximilien Vox and first cast by Deberny et Peignot in 1935.

R (p. 81): Graphic by Nicola Bailey, from a photograph of the staircase in the Can Prunera Museu Modernista, Majorca.

S (p. 85): From an anonymous engraved architectonic alphabet dating from the second half of the fifteenth century, reproduced in Jaro Springer, *Gothic Alphabets*, London (International Chalcographical Society) 1897.

T (p. 89): Graphic by Nicola Bailey, created from Fregio Mecano, a modular typeface designed in Italy in the 1920s and reproduced in Julian Rothenstein and Mel Gooding (eds.), *130 Alphabets and Other Signs*, London (Thames & Hudson) 1993, originally published by Redstone Press in 1991.

U (p. 93): From a London street sign composed of Minton Tiles 'Indestructible Lettering' by Minton Hollins & Co. Photo: Nicola Bailey.

V (p. 97): Graphic by Nicola Bailey.

W (p. 101): Nineteenth-century copperplate letter, reproduced in Pat Russell, *Decorative Alphabets Throughout the Ages*, London (Bracken Books) 1988.

X (p. 105): From Johann David Steingruber, *Architectonisches Alphabet*, Schwabach (Johann Gottlieb Mizler) 1773. © Victoria and Albert Museum, London.

Y (p. 109): Graphic by Nicola Bailey, composed of illustrations in *Mrs Beeton's Book of Household Management*, first published 1861.

Z (p. 113): Brutalist letter by Viacheslav Ivanov, Kazakhstan. Instagram: @viva_designer.

Cover and title page: Lettering inspired by a stencil alphabet thought to be by Edward Wright and reproduced in Julian Rothenstein and Mel Gooding (eds.), *ABZ: More Alphabets and Other Signs*, London (Redstone Press) 2003.

Endpapers: Graphic based on Charrette, a stencil typeface inspired by the lettering on Le Corbusier's drawings.

Typeface: Orbikular, designed by Mark Bloom, CoType Foundry, cotypefoundry.com.

Picture Credits

KEY
l = left, r = right, c = centre, t = top, b = bottom

© Architectural Association Archives: 111; © Arckit: 54; © Atelier La Juntana/RIBA Collections: 4bl (RIBA105676), 4br (RIBA105677); Philipp Wolff, 'Das neue Modell des Grabeskirche von Jerusalem in Stuttgart', *Illustrirte Zeitung* (Leipzig), vol. 40, 16 May 1863, p. 337. © Bayerische Staatsbibliothek München: 66; Codice Palatino 3 B 1.7, c. 37r. © Biblioteca Nazionale Centrale di Firenze: 75; © Bildarchiv Foto Marburg/fm134418 capital, Archaeological Museum of Epidaurus: 16; *L'Écume des jours*, © Brio Films/StudioCanal/Scope Pictures/France 2 Cinéma/Herodiade, 2013, Michel Gondry: 35; © DACS 2021, image courtesy of Drawing Matter Collections: 9b (DMC 1439); *Hævnens nat*, © Dansk Biograf Compagni, 1916, Benjamin Christensen: 34; © A. de Rijke/dRMM 2006: 55; © Dow Jones Architects: 18, 19; © dpa Picture-Alliance GmbH: 43; © Drawing Matter Collections: 6b (DMC 2081); © the architect, image courtesy of Drawing Matter Collections: 9tr (DMC 2584); © the estate of the architect, image courtesy of Drawing Matter Collections: 9tl (DMC 1500); © John Frazer/Architectural Association Archives: 27; © Lasdun Archive/RIBA Collections: 102 (RIBA4416), 103 (RIBA88114); © Library of Congress, Prints & Photographs Division, Balthazar Korab Collection, LC-KRB00-545: 83; © LSE Archives: 71; © Musée du Louvre, Inv. no. E 27111. Photo: Ulrike Fauerbach: 15; © Paul Raftery: 94; © RIBA Collections: 6tl (RIBA94461), 6tr (RIBA23373), 7t (RIBA28586), 7b (RIBA20855), 91 (RIBA127131), 107t (RIBA125761), 108t (RIBA126084); © RIBA Collections. Photo: Paul Robins: 107b (MOD/FRYR/1), 108b (MOD/WILLS/1); Location: Paris, Musée des Plans-Reliefs. © RMN-Grand Palais/Stéphane Maréchalle/René-Gabriel Ojeda: 59; © Royal Academy of Arts, London. Photo: Prudence Cuming Associates Limited: 51; © Roz Barr Architects: 46l, 46r; © Roz Barr Architects. Photo: Andrew Putler: 47l, 47r; © Agnese Sanvito: 95; © ScanLAB Projects: 98, 99; Courtesy of the Trustees of Sir John Soane's Museum, London, © Sir John Soane's Museum: 7c (M1242), 22 (vol. 85/XXXVIII); Courtesy of the Trustees of Sir John Soane's Museum, London, © Sir John Soane's Museum. Photo: Hugh Kelly: 23 (MR2); © Stanton Williams: 79t, 79b; © Technische Universität Berlin, 2019–2021: 87; © Tel Aviv Museum of Art. Photo: Nikos Magouliotis: 67; © Victoria and Albert Museum, London: 4t (A.10-1973), 5t (60755), 5b (E.955-2019), 8tl (IS.3-1999), 8tr (98-1870), 8b (CIRC.217-1916), 39 (73676), 63 (NCOL.2-2001), 115 (CD.15-2018); © Nigel Young/Foster + Partners: 31

Every effort has been made to trace and contact copyright holders of the illustrations reproduced in this book. The publisher will be happy to correct in subsequent editions any errors or omissions that are brought to its attention.

Index

Page numbers in *italic* refer to the illustrations.

ADEPT *4*
Alberti, Leon Battista 5, 19–20
Alessi, Galeazzo 75
Altieri, Giovanni 23–24, *23*
Amenemhat III, Pharaoh 15
Anchor Stone Building Sets 68, 90–91
ancient models 14–16
Anderson, John M. 116
Ando, Tadao *54*
Arckit *54*, 55
Aubert, Jean 9

Baalbek 16
Bailey, William 92
Barthes, Roland 68
Bartlett School of Architecture 56
Bauhaus 115
Bayko 92
Behr, Arnold 50
Belgrade Theatre, Coventry 79
Benjamin, Walter 40, 114
Bernini, Gian Lorenzo 75
Besançon *59*
Bild-O-Brik 92
Block Type A 56
Böhm, Gottfried 44
Borcherdt, Helmut 82
Boullée, Étienne-Louis 112
Boym, Constantin 8
Bradford, E.J. and A.T. 108
Brandani, Federico 74
Brickplayer 91
building kits 54, 55, 68, 90–92
Buontalenti, Bernardo 74, 76

Carême, Marie-Antoine 111–12
Carter, W.A.T. 92
Casebere, James 116
Catherine the Great, Empress 23
Chambers, Sir William 64
Chapelle Notre-Dame du Haut, Ronchamp 9
Charles II, King 96
Chichi, Antonio 23
Chiswick House, London *63*

Christensen, Benjamin 34
Church of the Holy Sepulchre, Jerusalem 64, 66–68, *66–67*
Church of the Light, Ibaraki, Osaka *54*
cities 94–96, 100
clay models 62, 64, 76, 107–108
Clement VII, Pope 23
Cöllen, Dieter 24
context models 95–96
Corbett, Harvey Wiley 115
cork models 8, 22–24

Demand, Thomas 116
Deutsches Architekturmuseum (DAM), Frankfurt am Main 52
digital modelling 26–28
dimensionality 71–72
donors' models 42
Dosio, Giovanni Antonio 76
double photography 115
Douglas, Mary 50
Dow Jones Architects 18–20, *18–19*
dRMM 55–56, *55*
Du Bourg, Richard 24

Easton Neston, Northamptonshire 6
École des Beaux-Arts, Paris 38–39
Edgeworth, Maria 90
Edgeworth, Richard Lovell 90
edible models 110–12
Egypt, ancient 5, 15, *15*, 22, 62
Eisenman, Peter 51, 116
Elgo Plastics 92
Eupalinos 16
exhibitions 30–32
Extinction Rebellion 56

films 34–36
Fischel, Victor A. 44
Fontaine, Pierre-François-Léonard 6
Foster, Norman *31*, 32, 64
Foster Associates 30–32
Fouquet, Jean-Pierre 8
Fowke, Captain Francis 76

Frajndlich, Abe 43
Frazer, John 26, *27*
Friedman, Yona 9
Friedrich II, Landgrave of Hesse-Kassel 23
Frings, Josef, Archbishop of Cologne 44
Fröbel, Friedrich 54, 68
Fry, Reginald C. 107–108, *107*
Fuller, Richard Buckminster 91

Galerie des Plans-Reliefs, Paris 59
Gandy, Joseph Michael 32
Garden Museum, Lambeth 19, 20
Gaudí, Antoni 26
Gehry, Frank 76
George III, King 24
Gillman, Derek 31–32
gingerbread houses 110–11
Glasgow School of Art 116
Gondry, Michel *35*
Google Earth 59, 95
Götz, Heinrich 88
Grand Tour 8, 23, 24
Graves, Michael 52
Great Pagoda, Kew Gardens 64
Greece, ancient 5, 15–16
Greenaway, Peter 112
Grimm, Brothers 110
Gropius, Walter 91
Guarini, Guarino 75
Guerra, Giovanni 76
gypsum 38–40

Hadid, Zaha *111*, 112
Hamilton, Sir William 24
hands 42–44
Harris, John 52
Hatakeyama, Naoya 116
Hawkins\Brown 56
Hawksmoor, Nicholas 6
Hedrich-Blessing 116
Hickok, Liz 112
Hitler, Adolf 35
Hornby, Frank 55
Huf Haus 56
Humperdinck, Engelbert 110
hyperrealism 115–16

IBUKU 5
Idlewild Airport, New York 82, *83*
Illinois Institute of Technology *43*
infrared light 106–107
Ingels, Bjarke 42–43
inspiration 46–48

Jahn, Helmut 42, 43
Jerusalem 66–68
Jewby, Paul 64
Johnson, Philip 43
junk 50–52
Juvarra, Filippo 74, 75

KAPLA 90
KEVA Planks 90
Kiddicraft 92
kits 54–56
Kliptiko 92
Klotz, Heinrich 52
Kockel, Valentin 24
Krayl, Carl 44
Ku.Be House of Culture and Movement, Frederiksberg *4*

Lambert, Phyllis 44
landscape 58–60
Lasdun, Denys 50–51, *51*, 52, 102–104, *102–103*
Le Corbusier 9, 42, 76, 114
Lebanon 16
Lego 54, 92
Leibovitz, Annie 43
Lévi-Strauss, Claude 50
light 103, 106–107
London 94–95, 95–96
London Airport 108, *108*
Lott's Bricks 91
Louis XIV, King of France 58
Luboń fertilizer production plant 87–88, *87*
Luckhardt, Wassili 44
Lynch, Kevin 50

Mackintosh School of Architecture, Glasgow 116
making models 62–64
maquettes 46–48, 78

materials, scale and 72
Matta-Clark, Gordon 51
Max Protetch Gallery, New York 51–52
May, Carl and Georg 24
Meccano 54, 55, 92
Medici, Cosimo de' 42
Medici family 75–76
Michelangelo 75–76
Mies van der Rohe, Ludwig 43–44, *43*, 52, 76, 114, 116
Minibrix *91*, 92
Mitchell, Arnold 91
Miyan Khan Chishti's Mosque, Ahmedabad *8*
Modernism 51, 114, 115
Moon, Karen 51
Moore, Charles 52
Moore, Gordon 98
Murtagh, Damien *54*
Musée des Plans-Reliefs, Paris 58, 59
MVRDV *4*, 42

Naked House 55–56, *55*
narrative 66–68
Nash, John *8*
National Theatre, London 50, *51*, *103*, 104
Network Modelmakers *63*
New London Architecture 94–95
Newlyn, Walter 71, *71*

OMA 42
one to one 70–72
Osman III, Sultan 67
Ott, Stephan 86
Otto, Frei 26
Ottoman Empire 66–68

Padiglione, Domenico 24
Paestum 24
Pallasmaa, Juhani 78
Palmyra *8*, 24
paper models *6*, 74–76
Paulius, James 92
Peak Leisure Club, Hong Kong *111*, 112
Pelet, Auguste 38
Penn, Irving 43
Perez, August & Associates 52

Peruzzi, Baldassarre 75
Phillips, Bill 71, *71*
photography 20, 114–16
pièces montées 111–12
Pieroni, Alessandro *75*, 76
Pinsent, Thomas *7*
Pipers Model Makers 94–96, *94*
Pitt House, Chudleigh Knighton *7*
plans-reliefs 58–60, *59*
plaster of Paris 8, 38, 48
Poelzig, Hans 44, 87–88, *87*
Polykleitos the Younger 16, *16*
Pompeii 23, 24
Pratt, Caroline 54
Pratt, Sir Roger 5–6
Premo Rubber Company 92
presentation models 35, 62–64
Price, Cedric 26
Proust, Marcel 40, 110
Pudu Mandapa, Madurai *8*

quick models 78–80

raking light 106
representation 82–84
Richardson, T.A. 76
Richter, F.A. 90
Riverwalk apartment complex, London *79*
Rogers, Richard 32, 64
Roman Empire 16, 22, 23, 38–39
Romanelli, Giovanni Francesco 76
Rome Innes, George *63*
Rosa, Agostino 23
Royal Academy of Arts, London 32, 104
Royal Albert Hall, London *4*, 76
Royal Institute of British Architects (RIBA) 50, 52
Roz Barr Architects 46–48, *46–47*
Ruegenberg, Sergius 44
Rupli, Kurt 35
Ruskin, John 112

Saarinen, Eero 82, *83*
Safdie, Moshe 92
St Anselm's Church, Kennington *18*
St Mary Magdalene's Church, Paddington 20
St Paul's Cathedral, London 5, *5*, 55
San Lorenzo, Florence 42, *75*, 76
Sanders, John 24
Sangallo, Antonio da the Younger 74
scale 70–72
ScanLab Projects 98–100, *98–99*
Schick, Conrad 66–67, 67–68
Schönberger, Angela 35–36
School of Oriental and African Studies (SOAS), London *102*
Segal, Walter 56
Sejima, Kazuyo 43
Selfridges, London *7*
Sharma Springs residence, Bali *5*
The Simpsons 111
simulations 36, 86–88
SITE 52
sketch models 62
Skyline 92
Soane, Sir John *7*, *7*, *22–23*, 24, 30, 32
Solari, Cristoforo 74
SOM 92
South Kensington Museum, London 39, *39*
Spear, J.W. & Sons 91
Speer, Albert 35
Stanton Williams 79–80, *79*
Stendhal 38
Stern, Robert A.M. 51
Stirling, James 32
Strasser, Susan 50
structural models 62
Studio Bark 56
study models 78–80
Süreyya Pasha 67

Tecton *102*, 103
Temple of Vesta, Tivoli *23*
Tholos, Epidaurus 16, *16*

Thurber, James 110, 112
timescale 71–72
Tirumala Nayak *8*
toys 54, 55, 68, 90–92
Trajan's Column 39–40, *39*
Trump, Donald 42

Uhl, Christian 87, *87*
ultraviolet (UV) light 106
urban models 94–96

Vacher's Model Bricks 90
Valer church, Norway 47–48, *47*
van den Boom, Holger 86
Vasari, Giorgio 23, 76
Venturi, Robert 52
Vian, Boris *35*
Victoria and Albert Museum, London *46*, 48; *see also* South Kensington Museum
Ville Spatiale *9*
virtual models 98–100
Vitruvius 5
Vkhutemas, Moscow 115, *115*

Webb, Aston 48
Wenebrik 92
WikiHouse 56
Williams, Sir Owen 108, *108*
Wines, James 52
Wood, Philip *102*, 103
wooden models 103–104
wooden toys 90
Wren, Sir Christopher 5, 30, 96
Wright, Frank Lloyd 91, 92

X-rays 107–108, *107–108*

yummy 110–12

zoom 114–16
Zuccari, Federico 76

First published 2021 by Merrell Publishers,
London and New York

Merrell Publishers Limited
70 Cowcross Street
London EC1M 6EJ

merrellpublishers.com

Published on the occasion of the exhibition
Shaping Space – Architectural Models Revealed,
The Building Centre, London WC1E 7BT,
24 September 2021–28 January 2022

Text copyright © 2021 the authors
Illustrations copyright © 2021 the copyright
holders; see p. 125
Design and layout copyright © 2021 Merrell
Publishers Limited

All rights reserved. No part of this publication
may be reproduced, stored in a retrieval
system or transmitted, in any form or by any
means, electronic, mechanical, photocopying,
recording or otherwise, without the prior
written permission of the publisher.

British Library Cataloguing in Publication
Data. A catalogue record for this book is
available from the British Library.

ISBN 978-1-8589-4697-9

Produced by Merrell Publishers Limited
Designed by Nicola Bailey
Project-managed by Claire Chandler
Proofread by Barbara Roby
Indexed by Hilary Bird

Printed and bound in China

T U V W
B C D E
J K L M
R S T U
Z A B C